HOLY FOOLS

THE LIVES OF TWENTY FOOLS FOR CHRIST

OSWIN CRATON

Illustrations by Emanuel Burke

ANCIENT FAITH PUBLISHING

CHESTERTON, INDIANA

Published by:
Ancient Faith Publishing
A Division of Ancient Faith Ministries
1050 Broadway, Suite 6
Chesterton, IN 46304

Unless otherwise noted, Scripture quotations are taken from the New King James Version, © 1979, 1980, 1982 by Thomas Nelson, Inc. Used by permission.

Cover art, St. Symeon of Emesa, by Emanuel Burke

ISBN: 978-1-955890-67-0

Library of Congress Control Number: 2024940257

Printed in the United States of America

CONTENTS

INTRODUCTION

T HEY WERE CALLED "FOOLS FOR Christ" (*uródivoi*)—those who had chosen a most difficult ascetic struggle (*podvig*) in order to glorify Christ and His Church and to instruct others as to the will of God.

Misunderstood, mocked, derided, spurned, abused, and often even beaten by their own people, these holy men and women were sources of divine mercy, guidance, and miracles—sometimes in their own lifetimes but often not until after passing from this life.

Just who were these "holy fools" and what purpose did they have with such an odd calling in service to their Lord Jesus Christ?

Some who read about the lives of these holy fools believe simply that they were people living with mental illnesses or challenges. While a few of those recognized as fools for Christ perhaps did genuinely suffer from mental illnesses or intellectual deficiencies according to today's standards, most are documented as having been in full possession of their faculties but as purposefully feigning their "foolishness" for the sake of Christ. Holy fools lived as icons of Christ, for Christ Himself appeared a fool to the world around Him—and does to this day. As Catherine Doherty asks in her book *Uródivoi*, "Can you imagine anything more foolish than voluntarily dying on a cross? . . . Is anything more foolish than spending years as a carpenter when

1

you are God?"[1] Christ bore ridicule, mocking, abuse, and ultimately death while proclaiming the will of God to humankind, and thus holy fools take that example to heart and bear similar ill treatment and humiliation in Christ's name. As Christ taught us all to have the heart of a child, the holy ones—even as fully mature adults—often cast off their "sophistication" to demonstrate a childlike heart that faced ridicule and rejection, believing that just as Christ was a fool in people's eyes, we too must have the courage to be foolish as He was. Saint Paul speaks of this foolishness extensively in his first epistle to the Corinthians:

> For Christ did not send me to baptize, but to preach the gospel, not with wisdom of words, lest the cross of Christ should be made of no effect. For the message of the cross is foolishness to those who are perishing, but to us who are being saved it is the power of God. For it is written: "I will destroy the wisdom of the wise, / And bring to nothing the understanding of the prudent." Where *is* the wise? Where *is* the scribe? Where *is* the disputer of this age? Has not God made foolish the wisdom of this world? For since, in the wisdom of God, the world through wisdom did not know God, it pleased God through the foolishness of the message preached to save those who believe. For Jews request a sign, and Greeks seek after wisdom; but we preach Christ crucified, to the Jews a stumbling block and to the Greeks foolishness, but to those who are called, both Jews and Greeks, Christ the power of God and the wisdom of God. Because the foolishness of God is wiser than men, and the weakness of God is stronger than men. (1 Cor. 1:17–25)

> Let no one deceive himself. If anyone among you seems to be wise in this age, let him become a fool that he may become wise. (1 Cor. 3:18)

---

1   Doherty, 11.

But even before Christ, we see prototypes of the fool for Christ—as far back as Old Testament times when several prophets of God adopted outlandish and even shocking behaviors in order to reveal His judgments. We see, for example, Isaiah walking naked for several years while he predicted Israel's captivity in Egypt (Is. 20:2–4); Ezekiel lying on his side for 390 days and eating bread baked over human dung (Ezek. 4:9–12); and Hosea marrying a harlot and buying her back from harlotry when she was unfaithful to him (Hos. 1:2; 3:1–2). It was St. Paul who first used the term "fools for Christ" in one of his epistles to the Corinthians (1 Cor. 4:10), pointing out that Christian doctrine and the Christian manner of life are foolish in the eyes of the world. In time, a number of Christian ascetics adopted the term and feigned foolishness or insanity in part to demonstrate the foolishness of the world about them, just as the prophets of old had done. These people feigned foolishness (mental illnesses) but in actuality were perfectly rational and in full command of all their senses. They adopted their behaviors in order to reject the status quo and cares of this world; to communicate (often in riddles or parables) great spiritual truths in admittedly sometimes outlandish ways (the equivalent of a slap in the face, which society often needs); and also to avoid the temptation of pride by allowing themselves to be humiliated, mocked, and sometimes even physically abused because of their seemingly absurd behavior.

So foolish behavior was not feigned merely for the sake of nonconformity but also to instruct and to portray deeper truths. To understand this, we can think of the example of kings, who sometimes employed professional "fools" or jesters to entertain them—and these same jesters, because of their profession of foolishness, were allowed to reveal truths to the king that would bring a harsh sentence to anyone else. In similar fashion, we read of many holy fools who awakened even kings, tsars, and emperors to errors of judgment and misguided behavior in order to set them back aright in God's eyes.

3

These holy fools were not perfect: not everything they did was necessarily hallowed and righteous. But like King David, they were nonetheless "after [God's] own heart" (1 Sam. 13:14), and He often blessed them with gifts of healing, clairvoyance, and other wonder-workings to attest to their sanctity. Many, like the prophets of old, were given the ability to see deeply into another's heart in order to discern their spiritual needs and to give instruction for their healing.

But there also are those fools for Christ who, by all accounts, may indeed have been mentally ill in some way. Why would the Church elevate mentally ill people to sainthood? While some people may consider elevating such individuals to sainthood an absurd idea, most of these saints demonstrated such profound faith and devotion to God that, despite their mental limitations, they truly showed forth both God's love and His power.

The Lord Himself told St. Paul that His "strength is made perfect in weakness" (2 Cor. 12:9), so God's wondrous power can shine forth from even our greatest infirmities. Consider also how the Lord had Gideon reduce his army to a mere 300 men so that the victory over the mighty Midianites could be seen clearly as a victory from God's arm and not from man's strength (Judg. 7). Further, Christ said that we must become as little children (Matt. 18:3), and at least in the eyes of the world many fools for Christ appear to be like children in maturity and intellect—though in reality they have been gifted with deep spiritual wisdom and insight. They are rightly elevated to sainthood by the Church.

So much emphasis has been placed on reason and intellect in our modern world that people who have various mental and intellectual challenges are considered almost subhuman. Some Protestant churches will not even allow people with these kinds of challenges to be admitted to their membership, thereby putting IQ as a condition of communion with Christ. But as Fr. Jordan Bajis has said, "One's ability to use his mind and faculties is not the requirement of faith. The orientation of one's heart and trust is the requirement."[2]

All human beings are capable of having this kind of faith, and anyone who has had a child or knows a person who struggles with mental illness can attest to this. A child or a person who has severe challenges may be unable to rationally comprehend the trust they have in their parent or caregiver, but there can be no question that trust is present—perhaps even in far greater measure than we "rational" people can muster. So even when a fool for Christ is not merely feigning his or her behavior but may actually suffer from some mental illness or intellectual challenge, we see that God can be glorified in His saints; and He can use even those of us whom others consider "broken" or "inferior" to proclaim His wonders, often granting miracles through these holy ones.

We all are called to be fools for Christ's sake—perhaps not in the extreme of those who bear the title "fool for Christ," yet we must maintain a holiness and purity of heart that would appear to be foolish in the eyes of the world about us. It is foolish to swim against the current of society, but we are called to do so. It is foolish to forgive and pray for those who abuse us, yet that is our task. It is foolish to stand for ancient truths when the contemporary world tells us they are outmoded or even evil; yet, as with Christ, we must maintain that which is "the same yesterday, today, and forever" (Heb. 13:8). It is foolish to feed and clothe the poor and outcast who can do nothing for us in return, especially when we ourselves have barely enough to sustain us; yet that is our calling. For we are called to be "fools for Christ" in multiple ways every day—even when not called specifically to outlandish behavior, our behavior is nonetheless outlandish to the world that surrounds us.

---

2   Bajis, *Common Ground*, 263.

NOTES

PLEASE NOTE THAT ALL DIALOGUE in these stories is paraphrased from other sources, unless otherwise indicated. Also, if you are interested in reading more about the lives of these saints, I have included a recommended reading section at the end of the book, as well as a bibliography that lists the sources I used for information that appears in these stories.

Additionally, all the feast dates (which you can find at the top of the page at the beginning of each chapter) in this book are New Calendar, and readers following the Old Calendar would need to subtract thirteen days from the date given.

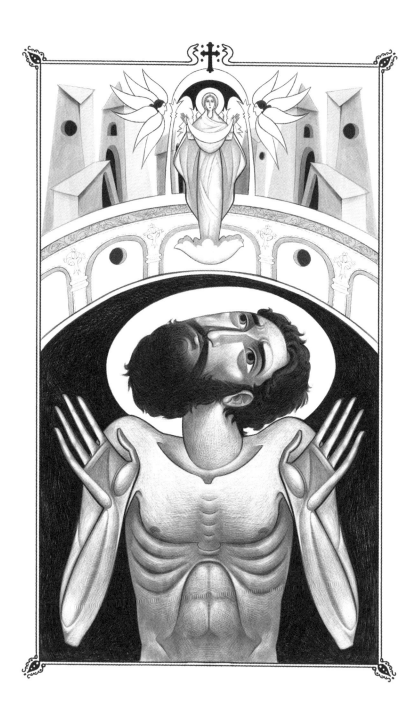

St. Andrew of Constantinople
(870-936)

BORN A SCYTHIAN, ANDREW WAS brought to Constantinople as a slave of Theognostus while still a small child. Theognostus was a *protospatharios* (an aristocratic title) of Emperor Leo VI and was quite well-to-do. He had Andrew baptized and taught him to read and write. Andrew excelled in his studies and was a skilled reader of Greek at a young age, particularly enjoying reading the lives of the saints whom he wished to emulate. Strongly dedicated to the Church, he became the spiritual child of one Nicephorus, a priest at Hagia Sophia.

Andrew desired to dedicate himself solely to God, and in his lifetime he received several visions that encouraged him in his path. His first recorded vision occurred while he was a young man. After standing in prayer intently for an extended period, he became weary and lay down to rest. In the vision he then received, he saw two armies facing each other, one an army of saints and the other an army of demons. A giant emerged from among the demons, and an angel descended from on high holding glorious crowns in his hand, which he told Andrew were for the one who could conquer the giant. Calling on the Lord for help, Andrew proceeded to do battle with the demon and after a great struggle was victorious. The Lord then said to Andrew, "Proceed with this good deed. Be a fool for My sake."[3] Andrew interpreted this to mean that he was being called to the great struggle of being a fool for Christ.

After this, Andrew began his podvig of playing the fool, which even his master Theognostus did not understand. Theognostus thought Andrew had become mentally unstable, and he took him to the Church of St. Anastasia—a place similar to a mental asylum where the insane were cared for—in search of a cure. However, instead of being "healed," Andrew's behavior only became more aberrant. By day he often howled like a madman, but at night he prayed to the Lord to ask whether his podvig was acceptable to Him.

One night St. Anastasia appeared to Andrew. She was accompanied by an elder, and the two were going about the grounds healing various people of their infirmities. When they approached Andrew, the elder asked St. Anastasia whether she would heal him as well, but she replied, "He needs no healing. He was healed by Him who said to him, 'Be a fool for My sake'"[4]—thus reaffirming him in his struggle as a fool for Christ. But because of his faked madness, he eventually was turned away from the church property and began living on the street. Greatly saddened at the apparent descent into insanity of his

---

3   "Blessed Andrew the Fool-For-Christ at Constantinople."
4   Novakshonoff, *God's Fools*, 11.

promising young scholar, Theognostus mercifully freed Andrew from slavery so that he could do as he willed.

After Andrew was driven away from the church grounds, he began behaving in a fashion common to many fools for Christ: he wandered the streets of Constantinople poorly clad and endured the scorn and mockery of people of all ranks. Once while he was walking by a brothel, he was pulled inside and taunted by the prostitutes who slapped him on the neck and tried to draw him into performing all manner of vile acts, but without success. Sometimes when he pretended to be drunk, he would be kicked, flogged, and spat upon. Andrew bore all these insults patiently, as though imitating the suffering of the Lord in His Passion, and he would forgive and pray for those who abused him.

He roamed the streets of Constantinople as a beggar, but whenever anyone would give him something he immediately would give it away to the poor. Because of this, even the poor came to despise him for being such a fool as to deny himself any of life's pleasures. He ate nothing but bread and water, and then only barely enough to sustain himself.

At the end of each day of playing the fool, he would spend the night in prayer, praying especially for those who had mistreated him during the day. Andrew would remove the mask of foolishness only for his spiritual father Nicephorus and for his disciple Epiphanius.

For his struggles, the Lord blessed Andrew with the gifts of wisdom and prophecy, and he offered spiritual help to many. Not all whom he counseled heeded his advice, however. It is said that once he encountered a graverobber as he was on his way to loot the grave of a wealthy woman who recently had died. Perceiving the robber's intent, Andrew warned him not to carry out his purpose, for if he did so he would never again see the sun or any human face. Ignoring the warning, the robber proceeded in his intent, though perplexed by how the fool had known his secret thoughts. After plundering the grave and preparing to exit the tomb, he felt what seemed to be a blow to his head and instantly was rendered blind. The robber lived out the rest of his days as a beggar on the streets and frequently regaled passersby with the prophecy of Andrew the Fool.

Others did take Andrew's counsel to heart. The story is told of a certain monk who had become overtaken by the sin of greed. Though very strict in his prayer life, when others would come to him for advice, he often would receive generous gifts from them. Rather than using these gifts to aid the poor, however, he became covetous of this wealth and hoarded it all for himself. When Andrew revealed to him the darkened condition of his soul, the monk then gave away all his riches and thereafter refused to accept any gift from others, telling them instead to give the money directly to those in need, saying, "Why should it be for me to distribute someone else's thorns?"[5]

On another occasion, Andrew was talking with his disciple Epiphanius when he received a vision in which a demon came and attempted to trap Epiphanius. But the demon would not approach Andrew and instead cried out, "You are my greatest enemy in all of Constantinople!" Rather than driving the demon immediately away, Andrew let him speak. "I feel," said the demon, "that the time is coming when my work here will be complete. When that time comes, men will be worse than I am now and children more skilled in wickedness than those who are grown. At that time I shall take my rest and do nothing more to tempt mankind, for they will do my will of themselves."

Andrew then asked the demon what sins gave his kind the most satisfaction, and the demon replied, "Idolatry, slander, evil against one's neighbor, sodomy, drunkenness, and love of money. These," he said, "give us the most joy." Andrew then asked the demon how his kind react when someone who had served them repents and turns away from their evil works. "It is hard to bear," replied the demon.

---

5   Novakshonoff, 15.

"We do all we can to bring him back. And many who have denied us and turned to God have come back to us!" At that, Andrew breathed on the demon, and he disappeared.

Andrew's best-known vision occurred while Constantinople was being besieged by enemy troops. Andrew and Epiphanius had joined a host of others at the Blachernae church to pray for deliverance. Sometime around the fourth hour of the all-night vigil, Andrew witnessed the Theotokos entering the church through the main door, accompanied by St. John the Forerunner and St. John the Theologian. They approached the amvon, at which point the Theotokos prayed and then entered the sanctuary and prayed again. Finishing her prayers, she removed her omophorion (stole), turned to the people, and spread out her omophorion over the faithful to protect them. Andrew, apparently unsure whether what he was witnessing was real, turned to Epiphanius and asked, "Do you see, brother, the Holy Theotokos, praying for all the world?" Epiphanius said, "I do see, Father, and I am in awe."[6] They witnessed her standing thus for a great while. After this vision, the army besieging Constantinople inexplicably withdrew and the city was saved. Thereafter the holy Feast of the Protection of the Theotokos was established and remains an important holy day in the Church to the present time.

Andrew reposed in the Lord in 936.

---

6   "Andrew the Fool-for-Christ."

St. Andrew of Totma
(1638-1673)

A NDREW WAS BORN INTO A devout but illiterate peasant family in Ust-Totma, Transvolga. He became educated by going to church and, after both his parents died, becoming a novice at the Galich Monastery. The abbot at the monastery was known for possessing great insight, and he encouraged Andrew to pursue the difficult podvig of becoming a fool for Christ.

Andrew therefore left the permanence of the monastery to become a wayfarer, wandering from village to village, but frequently returning to the Galich Monastery to meet with his spiritual father. On his elder's death, however, he settled near the Church of the Resurrection in Totma, a place where he was completely unknown. Here he practiced foolishness for Christ on an intense level, wandering the streets barefoot both summer and winter and eating only bread and water. Whenever anyone would give him anything, whether food or clothing, he would immediately give it away to the poor, keeping nothing for himself. Like so many other fools for Christ, Andrew would spend all night in prayer after playing the fool throughout the day.

For his great struggle, the Lord gave Andrew the gift of wonderworking. His gift became known among the people of the region, eventually reaching the ears of Azhibokai, the chief of an outlying tribe who was suffering from a disease of the eyes. He sought out Andrew and approached him one wintry day, offering Andrew a substantial amount of money to heal him. In response, Andrew turned and fled, not desiring the temptation to avarice or fame. Azhibokai possessed such faith, however, that he washed his eyes in the snow of Andrew's footprints and was healed of his infirmity.

God revealed Andrew's time of repose to him, and after making his confession and receiving the Holy Mysteries he lay down and fell asleep peacefully in the Lord in 1673, only thirty-five years of age. In his brief life he had attained a spiritual stature rarely seen even among the most ancient of Christians. When he died, it is said that the room where he lay was filled with a most wonderful fragrance.

Andrew's wonderworking did not cease with the end of his earthly life. He appeared some time later to a sick woman in a dream, holding before her the Gospel book, which he told her to venerate, and he told her to pray at his grave as well. When she awoke, she found herself healed. Many other miracles also were witnessed at his grave.

St. Basil of Moscow
(1468-1552)

B ASIL WAS BORN TO A poor family of serfs in the village of
Yelokhovo, which is now a suburb of Moscow. His parents were
childless and of advanced age when he was born, and they had prayed
for some time for a child, whom they vowed to dedicate to God. Tra-
dition has it that Basil's mother gave birth to him on the portico of
the church in Yelokhovo.

As a youngster, Basil was apprenticed to a shoemaker in Moscow,
and it was while working with him that he began exhibiting evidence
of saintly propensity even though he was still a child. One day an
itinerant merchant came into the shop and ordered a special pair of
leather boots that he wanted made to very precise specifications. He

informed the shoemaker that he would collect the boots the next time he was in Moscow the following year.

Before the merchant left, Basil began weeping and said to the merchant, "I wish you would cancel the order, since you will never wear them."[7] The statement stunned Basil's master, and he asked Basil what he meant by it. Basil explained to his master that the man would never wear the boots because he would die soon. This, as it turned out, is exactly what happened just a few days afterward. The master realized then that Basil was no ordinary boy.

Basil left home for Moscow proper when he was sixteen and began the difficult path of being a fool for Christ. He walked barefoot year-round and initially wore only a long shirt, whatever the weather. It seems that as he aged, or perhaps as what little clothing he had wore out, he would wear less and less, to the point that at least by old age he often went about the streets like the holy prophet Isaiah, totally naked. This he did in all purity of heart, having conquered the passions long before, and also because he had become truly dead to the world and possessed nothing of this sphere that would tie him to earth.

Like most fools for Christ, Basil wandered the streets and marketplaces often amongst the city's beggars and homeless, but despite being surrounded by people he practiced silence and prayed constantly. He also would behave in seemingly foolish fashion, once going through a marketplace and overturning a stand selling kolachi (a fruit-filled pastry) and spilling out a jug of kvass (a kind of cereal-based beer). For this the sellers thrashed the impudent young man, believing he was simply up to foolish mischief. Basil bore the beatings with joy and thankfulness. The merchants later discovered that the kolachi had been undercooked and the kvass was not properly prepared so that neither was fit for consumption. After incidents like

---

7   "Blessed Basil of Moscow the Fool-For-Christ."

these, Basil's reputation among the populace grew, and people began seeing him as a holy fool and man of God. People started coming to him for prayers and sometimes for advice.

Once a wealthy merchant was endeavoring to build a stone church in Moscow, but three times in the course of construction the arches collapsed and the building project was halted. In desperation, the merchant went to Basil for advice. Basil told him to go to Kiev and find one John the Cripple, and he would tell the merchant what was needed to fix the problem.

When the merchant finally found John the Cripple in a hut in Kiev, John was weeping and rocking an empty cradle. The merchant asked John who it was he thought he was rocking, since the cradle was empty. John replied, "I weep for my beloved mother, who was made poor by my birth and upbringing."[8] The merchant then understood that John was talking about the merchant's own mother, whom he had unlovingly put out of his house some time before. When the merchant returned to Moscow, he found his mother and welcomed her back into his home. After this, he was able to complete the building of the church without further incident.

Though Basil tried to conceal his holy life by foolishness, he nevertheless became so well known as a saint that he came to the attention of even the tsar himself (Tsar Ivan IV, "the Terrible") who held him in great esteem. The tsar went so far as to decree that no one was ever to harm Basil, and he both admired and feared him as an emissary of God.

Once when Tsar Ivan invited Basil to the royal palace, Basil was presented with a cup of wine which, instead of drinking, he poured out of the window. When the steward refilled his cup, Basil repeated the action. This happened three times, and the tsar began to grow angry at the perceived insult. Basil then told Tsar Ivan to

---

8   "Blessed Basil of Moscow the Fool-For-Christ."

allay his anger and said, "[K]now that by pouring out this drink I have extinguished the fire which is now consuming the whole city of Novgorod."[9] Basil then left the palace in a great hurry, and when the tsar's servants tried to follow him, they observed him walking across the Moscow River as if on dry land.

The tsar did not understand what Basil had meant by his actions or his statement, but he made note of the day and hour they occurred. He then sent a courier to Novgorod to see what was happening there, and when the messenger arrived the townsfolk told him that there indeed had been a fire in the city that was threatening to destroy it, but that they saw a naked man with a bucket putting out the flames. This had happened at precisely the day and time Basil had poured the wine out of Tsar Ivan's window.

Despite Ivan IV's penchant for adamantine and cruel behavior during his reign, incidents like this caused him to have great reverence for the saint. Basil was among the very few who could courageously chastise the tsar for his actions, encouraging him, as he did everyone of any station, to repentance and godliness.

Once during Lent the saint presented the tsar with a cut of meat (similar to the lesson St. Nicholas of Pskov gave him), saying that it did not matter whether Ivan fasted from meat since he was engaged in murder anyway, and that if he persisted in such violence it would doom his soul to hell.

On another occasion, after the tsar had attended Liturgy in the same church where Basil worshipped, Ivan encountered Basil and asked him where he had been. "There where you were," said Basil, "at the Holy Liturgy." Ivan then asked why he had not seen him there. (Basil had been standing in a corner where the tsar had not observed him.) Basil answered, "But I saw you and I saw where you really were . . . walking in thought on the Sparrow Hills and building your

---

ᴸonoff, *God's Fools*, 123.

palace."[10] Ivan then realized Basil knew that in his mind he had been thinking about a new palace he was having built on the Sparrow Hills along the Moscow River, rather than focusing on the divine service.

Sometimes Basil's lessons could be particularly severe in their warnings for repentance. A wealthy merchant once gave the nearly naked saint a costly crimson coat on a bitterly cold day—which Basil accepted only in order to make the giver happy. As Basil walked away, he was approached by two men who asked for his help. It seems that the two were in league with a third man who together had devised a plan to steal the costly garment for themselves. As one of the crew lay in the street pretending to be dead, the other two went to Basil to ask that he use his coat to cover the dead body. Basil, of course, having the gift of spiritual intuition, perceived their evil intent and sighed deeply in his heart. "Is your comrade truly dead?" he asked. "How long ago did he die?" After being told that he had just now died, Basil took off the garment and draped it over the "dead" man's body. He then stated, "Be henceforth dead forever for your wickedness, for 'the wicked shall be destroyed.'"[11] Basil then walked away unclad, despite the bitter cold, and the two thieves went to congratulate their accomplice on having achieved their goal. But the third man did not rise, for he was truly dead.

But to those who were in need of repentance yet had weaknesses difficult for them to control, Basil was most patient and compassionate. He frequented taverns, searching for a spark of goodness in the souls of those who languished there, encouraging all to find salvation.

As Basil would pass by different houses throughout the city, he could be seen sometimes throwing rocks at the corner of one house while weeping and kissing the corners of others. When people asked why he did this, he would say that he threw stones at some houses

---

10 Novakshonoff, 125.
11 Novakshonoff, 128–129.

in order to chase away the demons that were trying to gain entrance into holy dwellings, while at other houses he would weep along with the grieving angels outside who could not gain entrance because of the unholy things being done within.

Because he was beloved by rich and poor alike, people would often give Basil gifts. He would never keep anything for himself, however, but immediately would give everything to the poor. Once, though, this did not appear to have happened. When Tsar Ivan gave him a gift of gold, instead of distributing it to the poor and homeless he gave it to a well-dressed merchant. Many people were appalled at this and did not understand why he did it. But Basil explained that the merchant recently had lost everything and had not eaten in three days, and because of his fine clothing (all that he had left) he was not able to beg.

The righteous Basil reposed in the Lord on August 2, 1552 (some say 1557) and was mourned throughout Moscow by high and low alike. Saint Macarius, the metropolitan of Moscow, served his funeral, which was attended by throngs of people, including many nobles and clergy. So revered was St. Basil that Tsar Ivan IV himself served as one of the pallbearers. Basil was laid to rest in the cemetery of Trinity Church, where in 1554 the Holy Protection Cathedral was built. The Protection church later was renamed in honor of St. Basil and is now one of the most-recognized structures on Red Square in Moscow.

St. Domna of Tomsk
(† 1872)

DOMNA (KARPOVNA) WAS BORN TO a wealthy and noble family in Ukraine sometime in the early 1800s. She was orphaned at an early age and was brought up by her aunt. The aunt provided Domna with an excellent education so that she learned to read and write very well and spoke several different languages. She was reportedly a beautiful young woman who had many suitors, but she desired to devote herself wholly to Christ and preserve her virginity for His sake. Her relatives planned nonetheless to force her into marriage, and when she learned of their intention she secretly stole away from the house with nothing more than the clothes on her back and began a pilgrimage to various holy places.

While traveling to one of the holy sites, she was arrested by the police because she had no papers on her to validate who she was. Considered a vagrant, she was exiled to Siberia under the name Maria Slepchenko. When she arrived in Siberia, she settled in the city of Tomsk. It was there that she took up the struggle of becoming a fool for Christ.

Though she chose Tomsk as her place of residence, in reality she had no specific corner to call her own but typically spent both day and night outside, even during the bitter cold of winter. She would dress herself in various items of clothing she might find discarded, and she carried with her several cloth bags that hung about her in which she would put assorted items that she would happen upon randomly—broken glass, candles, rope, string, shoes, etc. In many ways she resembled what we today would call a "bag lady," though differing from most by remaining in a constant state of prayer. Often, instead of using a prayer rope, she would use the various items in her bags to count her prayers.

The local citizens came to revere her for her piety, humility, and kindness toward others and would give her warmer clothing during the bitter cold winters. These she would accept with great gratitude, but within a few hours she would be found shivering again, having given her warmer outerwear to others suffering from the cold.

When she learned of the sad state of most prisoners in the local jail, she began to frequent the jail in order to pray for and encourage those within. She would walk among them singing hymns and praying. As the police were suspicious of such behavior, they eventually arrested her as well, but when the local citizens learned of it, they brought all manner of food and tea to the jail in her support. These gifts Domna never kept for herself, but retaining the same giving attitude she had exhibited in the streets of Tomsk, she doled them out amongst the prisoners instead.

When finally released again, Domna continued to wander the streets as before, befriending not only the poor and needy but also the stray animals within the city. She would care for and even feed them, especially the dogs, who became her constant companions. Frequently she could be found at night surrounded by a throng of dogs who no doubt expressed their gratitude to her by keeping her warm on cold Siberian winter nights. Even when in the presence of animals, Domna could be heard continuing in her unceasing prayer. Because of her great love and care for all of God's creatures she often is pictured with dogs in icons.

Though she prayed without ceasing throughout the day and night, it is said that her prayers intensified when she was in a church. But it was only when she thought no one else was close by that she would pray with such depth from the heart and with tears, for whenever she perceived that someone was watching she would resume to play the fool, singing, putting out candles, and taking some of the candles and putting them in her bags.

For her struggles, the Lord gave her the gift of clairvoyance, and she gave much spiritual counsel to others. The people of Tomsk grew to love Domna, and she loved much in return.

She fell asleep in the Lord on October 16, 1872, and was buried in the Convent of St. John the Forerunner in Tomsk. The exact location of her grave became lost after the ungodly Communist regime closed the monastery and destroyed its cemetery, but a chapel dedicated to St. Domna was built in 1996 over the supposed location of her grave. Locally she is thought of as the "Siberian Xenia of Petersburg."

St. Feofil of the Kiev Caves
(1788-1853)

O N A CHILLY OCTOBER DAY in 1788, in the village of Makh-
novo near Kiev, Evfrosiniya Gorenkovsky gave birth to twin
boys. The older twin was named Foma and the younger Kalliniky.

As in the story of the twins Jacob and Esau, Kalliniky was loved
but Foma hated by his mother. Never bonding with him as she
desired, Evfrosiniya grew to despise the infant Foma to the point that
she asked her servant to take him secretly to the river at dawn before
anyone was about and drown him. The servant begged Evfrosiniya
not to ask her to commit such an abomination, but Evfrosiniya
was insistent.

Before dawn one morning, the servant carried Foma in her arms
to the river's edge and there, weeping and making the sign of the

cross over the child, she dropped him into the river. To her great astonishment, the baby did not sink and drown as she expected but floated to the surface of the water and was wafted to the other side of the river where he came to rest on the dry riverbank. The servant was amazed at such a thing, but to fulfill her mistress's command lest she be thrashed for disobedience, she crossed over to the other side and threw Foma back into the river again. But once more the child was saved from drowning and was carried by the current to a small island in the river where, sleeping peacefully, he was delivered again onto dry land.

The servant was awestruck by this double miracle and could no longer bring herself to cause harm to the baby. Collecting him from the island, the servant returned to her mistress and described the miraculous deliverance God had granted to Foma. The servant insisted that attempting to harm the child further would bring about judgment from God and that they should have nothing more to do with that evil plan. But Evfrosiniya's heart was so hardened against her child that she took the baby from the servant's arms and set out for the river herself, the servant following secretly behind.

Before reaching the river, Evfrosiniya passed a mill near the house. As it was still early morning and no one was about, she decided to place Foma under the mill wheel so that he would be crushed to death as the wheel turned. But as she walked away, suddenly the millstone stopped turning. With no turning wheel, the water pressure built up significantly and created a very loud roar, which drew the attention of the miller. When he inspected the millstone, he saw the infant floating in the water at its base and lifted him up to safety. As soon as he did so the wheel resumed turning normally.

When the servant girl saw this third miraculous deliverance of the infant Foma, she began to weep bitterly over her sin. She went to the miller and told him everything that had happened that morning. The miller knew that returning the child to his murderous mother would

32

be intolerable, so he instead took the child to its father, Andrei, who had not been privy to his wife's evil intentions. Andrei took pity on the child and placed him in the care of a local wet nurse. This kind woman cared for Foma as if he were her own son. But soon Andrei became ill and, perceiving death close at hand, asked the miller to care for Foma after his repose.

News of the miracles surrounding this small boy spread throughout the surrounding region, and a wealthy peasant who was childless heard about Foma and begged the miller to allow him to care for the boy. Out of concern for the child's best interest, the miller agreed, since the peasant was better able to provide for the child's needs.

From boyhood Foma was regarded as being "different." Instead of playing, he often would be seen sitting by himself as though contemplating life and its mysteries. He loved going to church and would never miss a service. He fasted assiduously even while very young and was intense in his prayer life, always praying for his mother and that her heart would be softened toward him.

When he learned that his mother had been diagnosed with a terminal illness, he decided to visit her in person. Not knowing what kind of reception he might receive, he trusted that his prayers had been able to achieve some success in mending her heart. He found that indeed this had happened, and Evfrosiniya wept profusely and begged Foma's forgiveness. She embraced Foma in love and made the sign of the cross, then fell asleep in death. Foma closed her eyes with his own hands.

Foma proved to be exceptionally bright and excelled in his studies, but after finishing the academy he chose not to pursue higher education but instead desired to spend more time in church. He went first as a reader to a parish in Chigirin, but since his voice was rather poor, he was sent instead to be a sacristan in the village of Obukhov.

Not long afterward he began contemplating a monastic life, and in 1812, at age twenty-four, he entered the Bratsky Monastery in

Kiev as a novice. He was tonsured a monk in 1821 and given the name Feodorit. A year later he was made a deacon, a position that came with a small income, but he gave all his money to the poor, saying, "What is it to me, this flesh and blood, which one day will turn to dust?"[12]

In 1834, Feodorit took the schema and was renamed Feofil. At this time, he took upon himself the difficult podvig of being a fool for Christ. Dead to the world and its passions, Feofil would spend his days and nights in prayer and deep devotion, not even allowing himself to become too close to any other individual for, as St. Nikolai Velimirović would later put it, friends can bind one to earth, whereas Feofil sought to demolish all his aspirations in the world.

Just as he had done since childhood, Feofil never missed a service at church, though he typically would remain at the church doors or just inside rather than taking a place further within the sanctuary. He always carried with him some type of container—whether a basket, bowl, or bucket—in which he kept various provisions that he would distribute to the poor. Beyond that, his only other possessions were a small Psalter that he read continually and a coffin he had placed in his cell which was filled with food and other items to give to people in need.

One of his daily routines was to go to the river each morning to get water. Sometimes he would get in one of the boats tied nearby and row across to the other side of the Dnieper River where he would go into the woods and spend time in prayer. He then would bring the boat back when he returned to his cell. He always would take whatever vessel he found, and the owners never complained but rather felt blessed.

One morning when he went to get water, he encountered a young postulant from the nearby Florovsky Monastery. Sisters from the

---

12   Sanidopoulos, "Saint Feofil."

monastery sometimes would come to draw water from the Dnieper because it was high in iron and considered healthier than their normal water. But before anyone from the Florovsky Monastery would come to the Dnieper, they were to seek permission from their superior. In her haste, this young postulant left before doing so. When she attempted to get water into her bucket she lost her balance, and while rescuing herself from a plunge into the river she dropped the key to her cell, which she had been holding in her hand.

As Feofil approached he saw her weeping despondently. When he asked why she was weeping, she explained that she had lost the key to her cell in the river and did not know how she would explain that to her superior. Feofil said, "It serves you right, silly. The next time you won't go without a blessing." Then he asked for the bucket, stooped and filled it with water, and handed it back to the postulant, saying, "Here. Take this and go home. You have your water and your key."[13] And when the postulant looked into the bucket, she saw her lost key. She turned to thank Feofil for this miracle, but he was nowhere to be seen.

Because Feofil was so dead to the world, his behavior sometimes annoyed the monks and those who came to see him. Though God recognized his righteousness, others did not always understand the point of his behavior. Students from the academy would hold conversations with him to mock him, but seeing their intent, he would shoo them away. One student, however, a Pyotr Krychanovsky, revered Feofil and sought to emulate his podvig. It was to Pyotr that Feofil gave his famous advice on how to respond to others' unjust criticisms: "Do not listen to them," he said. "Behave like a dead person who does not respond to anything surrounding him [sic]. If you are praised—be silent. If you are scolded—be silent. If you incur losses—be silent. If you receive profit—be silent. If you are satisfied—be silent. If you

---

13   Znosko, *Hieroschemamonk Feofil*, 18.

are hungry—also be quiet. And do not be afraid that there will be no fruit when all dies down; there will be! Not everything will die down. Energy will appear—and what energy!"[14]

Even some of the monks in the monastery were antagonistic toward Feofil, not only because of his unusual behavior but also because of his attire. He never buttoned his monastic robe and let it get dirty and stained with oil from cooking for others. He sometimes would kneel on a large tree stump in prayer for days at a time, and his apparel would grow more and more bedraggled. On his feet he wore torn slippers or sometimes mismatched boots. Like St. Isidora, he would tie a dirty towel around his head. Once, to bring attention to the sin of gluttony amongst the monks, he walked about the monastery courtyard with a large down pillow stuffed beneath his garment in order to appear a corpulent gormandizer himself.

Once the monks decided to play a prank on Feofil. When Feofil left the church one morning to walk and pray through the cemetery, the monks noticed that he had left his cherished Psalter behind. (Feofil had it memorized anyway.) One of the monks took the Psalter and hid it in his pocket as a joke. When Feofil came back into the church, he did not go to where he had left his Psalter but went immediately up to the monk who'd taken the precious book. Looking him in the eye he said, "Oh elder, elder. You must die tomorrow and you play evil tricks today."[15] And just as Feofil foretold, that same monk passed suddenly the following day.

Feofil would never travel by carriage but on a cart drawn by a small horse. Since it was not possible to keep a horse at the monastery, a local peasant gifted a small horse to Feofil and cared for it himself, bringing it every day to the monastery already watered and fed. Feofil would sit in the little wagon pulled by this tiny horse and read his

---

14   Znosko, 22.
15   "The Life of St. Feofil, Fool-for-Christ of Kiev."

Psalter. Often rude boys would chase after him, mocking and even throwing rocks at him for being a "mad monk." In response, Feofil would only occasionally glance at them and shake his finger, then go back to reading his Psalter. Later, at the hermitage, he would have a bull that would pull a small cart in the same way. Often a bull is written in his icon to this day.

The monks who protested Feofil's behavior finally convinced the metropolitan to agree to having him removed, and he was transferred to the Novopasyechny Orchard to care for the grove. Feofil enjoyed the solitude there, but it was a considerable distance for him now to walk to church. Despite that, he never missed a single service, being as diligent as in his youth.

Less than a year after he moved to the orchard, Feofil was transferred yet again, this time to the Kitayevskaya Hermitage outside of Kiev (also known as the Kiev Caves). Here he increased his podvig as a fool for Christ. For his acts of foolishness, the superior of the hermitage despised him, as did the sacristan Polykarp. Polykarp often would confront Feofil and even beat him, but the saint would only stand quietly before him with his hands folded and accept the abuse. He also was moved from cell to cell out of spite, but each time he would, without question or argument, simply gather his mantle, an icon, and his Psalter and move to the appointed cell.

A strict faster, Feofil ate very little, and what he did consume from the refectory kitchen he would mix together in one dish, disregarding the fact that there often would be both sweet and bitter flavors. "It is the same in life," he would say, "both bitter and sour and salty mixed with sweet and all this must be digested."[16]

Having been blessed with the gifts of discernment and clairvoyance, Feofil was able to predict many events that were to come to pass and also to reveal secret troubles in the hearts of those who came to

---

16   Znosko, 43.

see him, leading many to repentance and salvation. A number of healings of physical infirmities also are recorded as having been worked through the righteous Feofil.

Once a married noblewoman came to him and asked him for a blessing. She was very beautiful and came wearing a new silk dress. When the saint asked again if she wanted his blessing, he then told her to hold up the hem of her dress. Thinking that he perhaps would put some herbs or flowers in the skirt, she was shocked when he proceeded to pour a bowl of cabbage soup into her dress instead. But before she could speak, he said, "You are unfaithful to your husband daily! And who would come to ask me for a blessing wearing a silk dress? Because you seduce young men with your beauty, I will give you a good chiding!"

On another occasion a lady landowner came asking to meet with Feofil, and he was out tilling the garden wearing only his undershirt. The lady was appalled. Feofil then came up to her and asked, "Why have you stripped your serfs down to their last shirt? Why do you let them go without bread? You have no conscience about ruining people, but before a humble monk you express shame? Repent of your excessive pride! Love those near you lest you stand naked and shameless before God's judgment!" This so struck the lady to her heart that she leapt from her carriage with tears of repentance and begged for forgiveness, thus amending her prideful ways.

In April of 1853, Feofil was transferred once more to Goloseyevo at the request of the superior of Goloseyevskaya Monastery who felt that the aging saint would be more comfortable there. Feofil accepted this transfer, as all the ones previous, with humble obedience and said, "Let it be as you wish. I'll return to my old place to die."[17]

During his final days on this earth, Feofil spoke more freely to others and expounded a deep knowledge of Scripture. His message

---

17   Znosko, 112.

focused often on love: "Love one another with a sacred love," he would admonish, "and do not hold anger against each other."[18] Shortly before his death, he asked that someone go to the belfry and retrieve a long wooden box that had been used to store candles and bring it to his cell. In this he asked to be buried. On the morning of October 28, he received the Holy Mysteries for the final time and was at peace. Shortly before Vespers, he instructed one of the attendants, Dmitry, not to leave the cell today because he would see something truly extraordinary.

After having the attendants light the votive lamp before the icons and sprinkle incense on the coals, Feofil lay on the bench and told one of the other attendants to go and tell the superior, "Feofil has demised; toll the bell."[19] They both ran to the saint's cell and found that he indeed had fallen asleep in Christ.

Dmitry had remained in the cell with Feofil after the other attendant had left, and he related what had happened. He said that at the moment of the saint's death, the roof of the cell rose up and the blue sky reached down as if to receive the holy soul of the righteous Feofil. When he had yielded his spirit to God, the room returned to normal.

Countless miracles were performed through Feofil during his life, and they continue to be performed even to this day.

---

18 Znosko, 114.
19 Sanidopoulos, "Saint Feofil."

St. Gabriel of Mtskheta
(1929-1995)

GABRIEL WAS BORN GODERDZI URGEBADZE in Tbilisi, Georgia, USSR, on August 26, 1929. His father, Vasily Urgebadze, was an official in the Communist Party and was murdered in 1931 under mysterious circumstances—likely a victim of Stalin's purges. After his father's death, his family began calling Goderdzi by the name Vasiko as a means of honoring his father's memory.

Fatherless at age two, Vasiko's childhood occurred during a time and place where religious persecution was astonishingly severe. Though his mother had him baptized in infancy, for fear of the atheist regime's brutal treatment of any who professed religious beliefs openly, she did not instruct the young lad in the faith for his own protection.

One day when he was seven, Vasiko overheard his neighbors quarreling, and one of them yelled at the other, "You have crucified me like Christ!"[20] The young Vasiko did not know what "crucify" meant, nor did he know who "Christ" was, so he asked grown-ups to explain. Being too terrified to speak openly about such matters for fear of the communists, the adults simply told him to go inquire at a church. Vasiko went to a local church and asked the warden what the terms meant. The warden explained to him in simple terms about the sacrifice of Christ on the Cross and advised him to read about it in the Gospel. Vasiko saved his money (mostly by skipping school breakfasts) and bought a copy of the Gospel from a church shop. He kept this precious book with him to the end of his life.

Vasiko read and reread the Gospel book many times as a young boy and practically had it memorized. Even at such an early age he decided that he wanted to live his life for Christ and, much to his mother's displeasure, he lost interest in everything except the Gospel.

Vasiko would find icons in trash heaps where people had discarded them in fear of the secret police discovering them in their homes. These he would collect, clean, and place in his icon corner in his bedroom, and he would pray before them at length each night before going to bed. He related later in life that on one such night he sat quietly after prayer in his room when he heard a voice inside him telling him to look up at the sky. He went to his balcony and looked up and saw a large cross in the sky. This he later came to realize was to reveal to him the cross that he would be called to bear for his love of God and the people.

Because Vasiko lived a holy life in the midst of a thoroughly anti-Christian world, God granted him the gifts of clairvoyance and wonderworking at an early age. It is said that one day Vasiko was cleaning large stones away from the abandoned church of St. George.

---

20   Khrustaleyva, "Elder Gabriel."

As his uncle passed by, Vasiko greeted him and asked him to come help him move one particularly large stone. His uncle wrestled with the stone for some time but was unable to budge it. Vasiko then said, "In the name of Christ!"[21] and took up the stone by himself and set it down with the rest of the rocks he had removed. Witnessing this miracle, his uncle reaffirmed his own faith in Christ from that day forth.

By the time he was twelve, Vasiko had grown to be known for his gift of clairvoyance. This was during World War II, and many local citizens came to him out of concern for relatives fighting at the front. Vasiko's ability to relate important news to others led many to turn their hearts back to the church. But being recognized for possessing this special blessing from the Lord troubled Vasiko because he did not wish any praise to be given to him but to Christ alone. To avoid receiving his neighbors' acclaim, he would engage in foolish behavior, such as putting himself in the garbage and repeating loudly, "Always remember Vasiko, that you are garbage and never think highly of thyself!"[22] His family would sometimes punish him for such things, but he persisted and encouraged others to mock and insult him in order to avoid any temptation to pride.

During this period of governmental persecution, many people would hide their icons in various places in their houses (or sometimes throw them out, as has already been mentioned). Once the icons were hidden away, some people would grow forgetful and fail to reverence these holy items as they should. Vasiko often would approach people and remind them that they had such-and-such icon hidden away, and even tell them where it was hidden, and he stressed to them the importance of reverencing the icons properly; and if they didn't want to do that, he asked them to give him the icon, which he then would take and care for appropriately. Many of these cherished icons may

---

21 Transfiguration Orthodox Church of Samtavro, "Archimandrite Gabriel Urgebadze."

22 Sanidopoulos, "Saint Gabriel the Confessor."

still be seen today by those who make pilgrimages to the saint's cell in Samtavro Convent.

Although twelve-year-old Vasiko came to be highly respected by his neighbors for his deep devotion and spiritual gifts, his mother attempted to discourage his religiosity. Knowing what kinds of persecution he likely would face, and also being disturbed by his "strange" behavior as a child, she insistently pleaded with him to abandon his faith and be like the other boys his age. At one point she became so distraught that she threw his Gospel book into the toilet, but Vasiko hastily retrieved it and pressed it close to his breast, weeping sorrowfully.

This episode forced the young saint to make a life-changing decision. Late that same night, he crept out of his house and began walking. After several days he arrived at the Samtavro Convent in Mtskheta. Over the next few weeks, he took refuge in various monasteries, eventually settling for a time in Bethany Monastery where two monks, Fr. George and Fr. John, became his dearest father confessors.

After he left Bethany, he seems to have wandered about to places unknown, but he was given refuge at one point in Tbilisi, in the home of a fortune teller. Vasiko was very grateful for the kindness of the woman, but it pained his heart to see her earning her living in such a sinful occupation. When the fortune teller became ill one day, Vasiko stood in for her to her clients, but instead of pretending to read their fortunes he spoke to them each about the love of God and encouraged them in the Christian life. His gift of clairvoyance also gave him opportunities to speak with each about hidden sins in their lives and to warn them of future dangers. He roused in them the need to go to Confession and to receive the Holy Eucharist, which many did.

Word of this strange young boy who could reveal secret sins spread and eventually came to the ears of Vasiko's mother, who had mourned his departure grievously. When she found him, she begged him to return home, promising that she would no longer prohibit his living for Christ but would let him live as he wished. Vasiko returned home and obeyed his mother, but he continued daily in his prayers and the studying of the Gospel. He also helped his stepfather in his bakery during this time.

When Vasiko turned twenty in 1949, he was called up for mandatory military service, to which he dutifully submitted. But even while in service surrounded by atheists and anti-religion zealots he maintained his faith, often sneaking away whenever possible to visit holy sites near where he was deployed. Eventually the military discovered his faith, and after they dismissed him from service he was declared mentally ill (because communists thought only a mentally ill person would believe in God). He returned home and built a small chapel in his backyard. He wished to enter a monastery—of which there were but few remaining open—but the communist government made entry into monastic life an exceedingly difficult proposition.

Finally, in 1954 he entered the Kutaisi Motsameta Monastery in Georgia and was tonsured a monk with the name Gabriel. He eventually was ordained a deacon, and later, a priest. In 1960 he began serving in the Bethany Monastery with his greatly beloved spiritual father, Fr. George. But after Fr. George died two years later, the Soviet government closed Bethany Monastery, and Gabriel returned once again to his childhood home in Tbilisi and began a small parish in the little chapel he had built behind his house.

The incident in Gabriel's life that is perhaps best known throughout the world, both secularly and within the Church, occurred in 1965 during the May Day celebration of Soviet might. May 1 happened to fall on Holy Saturday that year, and a great parade proceeded through the streets immediately after Fr. Gabriel had just served the Divine Liturgy. As he walked along the street, he saw a giant, twenty-six-foot picture of Vladimir Lenin adorning a building with the caption "Glory to Great Lenin." Gabriel walked up to the giant picture and set it on fire. He then turned to the astonished crowd and began preaching to them, warning them that they were bowing down before idols and that glory belongs not to the corpse of Lenin but to the conqueror of death, Jesus Christ.

As in the days of the holy apostles, the crowd was not receptive to his words but descended on him in fury, beating him mercilessly and—again, like in days of old—literally stoning him. To quell the uprising, Soviet authorities moved in and rescued Gabriel, but not before he was near the point of death. They took him to a nearby hospital, where he was found to have no fewer than seventeen broken bones, including a fractured skull. He was sentenced to death for his action, but when his case became known and publicized by Western media, the sentence was rescinded and instead he was declared a schizophrenic psychopath and was imprisoned in a psychiatric hospital, from which he was released seven months later. Perhaps due to governmental pressure, Fr. Gabriel was suspended from all priestly duties and thereafter attended Liturgies as a layman. He returned yet again to his mother's home in Tbilisi.

Despite being classified mentally ill, Soviet authorities would call him in to interrogate him time and again. He often would return from these interrogations badly beaten, even to the point of not being able to walk on his own, but he endured it all.

One day his sister heard him weeping dolefully in the chapel in his backyard. She assumed he was weeping because of all the trials and tortures he had had to endure in his life, but when she asked him why he was crying he replied that he wept because "Christ was born in a lowly manger; yet, people show me respect and kiss my hand."[23]

Gabriel was greatly troubled when people elevated him. Perhaps because of that, he resolved around this time to adapt wholeheartedly to the podvig of a fool for Christ. He began preaching openly and loudly in the streets and started drinking wine (which he previously

---

23   "Archimandrite Gabriel Urgebadze."

had never touched), often pretending to be drunk. This was to diminish people's opinions of him so that all glory should go to God. He is even quoted as explaining why he often behaved as a fool: "When it seemed to me that I was an important person or that I was better than others, I would act that way (foolishly); and when people would laugh at me I'd be humbled and see that I'm garbage."[24]

His antics as a fool were never for mere show, but he designed them for the singular purpose of helping lead others to a closer walk with Christ. Once when he was visiting a monastery, he passed by several priests who were seated on a bench in the courtyard. Gabriel stopped and then pranced in front of them in a silly dance. Several of the priests were aghast at such behavior until they realized that somehow Gabriel knew that the night before they all had secretly dressed in street clothes and attended a nightclub together.

On another occasion, in confession Gabriel instructed a penitent to go out and buy a pornographic magazine. At first he was indignant at such a penance, but the man soon remembered that he had hidden several pornographic photos in his office at work and had not mentioned them in his confession. He then realized that Fr. Gabriel's instruction was a call for him to come to full repentance.

In the early 1980s Gabriel relocated to the Samtavro Convent, where he lived in a former chicken coop. Though the building provided no protection from the harsh winter winds, Gabriel refused to leave or accept warmer clothing for himself. Instead, he frequently could be seen outside the coop in prayer standing barefoot and covered with ice and snow.

In the last years of his life, Gabriel spoke principally of the necessity of loving God and one's neighbor, for "God is love. Do as much good as you can. . . . Be humble, for God sheds his grace on the

---

24   Pehanich, "St. Gabriel Urgebadze."

humble. Love one another, for without love no person will enter the doors of Paradise."[25]

He suffered greatly in his final days, unable to walk or get up to prepare food for his guests as he always had done with his own hands. His final words were recorded as, "I have followed you, Christ, from [age] twelve. . . . I am ready, take me!"[26] He reposed peacefully on November 2, 1995, and was buried not in a coffin but wrapped in a simple sackcloth shroud. Many miracles have been recorded as taking place at his grave.

25 Obitel-Minsk Team, "Saint Gabriel of Samtavro."
26 Sanidopoulos, "Saint Gabriel the Confessor."

St. Isidora of Tabenna
(fourth century)

O NE OF THE EARLIEST RECORDED practitioners of the ascesis of foolishness for Christ's sake is Isidora of Tabenna. She
lived in the fourth century in the monastery of Tabenna in Egypt, an
ascetic community St. Pachomius the Great had founded.

Feigning insanity, Isidora was largely despised by the 400 nuns
at the monastery and was relegated to performing the most menial
tasks. She spent most of her time in the kitchen, scouring the floor
and washing dishes. So willing was she to perform any lowly task, the
sisters began referring to her as "the monastery sponge."

Isidora did not wear a traditional cowl, but instead she covered
her head only with an old rag. Whatever task she was asked to do
she did with all her might, maintaining always the spirit of Christ in

everything she put her hands to. Even when she suffered abuse from the sisters she served—which she often did—Isidora never once was heard to complain or become angry. The sisters considered her insane or demon-possessed and refused even to eat with her, not understanding Isidora's desire to fulfill the words of St. Paul: "Let no one deceive himself. If anyone among you seems to be wise in this age, let him become a fool that he may become wise" (1 Cor. 3:18).

In all the years Isidora was at the monastery, no one ever remembered seeing her eat a meal since she satisfied her need for sustenance by eating the leftovers on the plates she washed and drinking the filthy dishwater. In all of this, she constantly maintained a spirit of contentment, humility, and love.

At the same time, a number of miles away in the Porphyrite desert there dwelt a holy anchorite by the name Pitirim. Living in solitude, Pitirim was known far and wide for his ascetic struggles, having been a disciple of St. Anthony the Great. Sometimes he was tempted by pride to consider himself superior to others. One day an angel appeared to him and said, "What makes you think that your struggles are so excellent? Would you like to see a woman more devout than yourself? Go to the [women's monastery in Tabenna], and you will find a nun wearing a rag on her head. She is superior to you because she gives herself up to struggle in the midst of people; she serves everyone and though everyone mocks and reviles her, she has never looked away from God with her heart. But you, sitting here in the desert, are sinning with your thoughts in the city."[27]

Humbled by these words, Pitirim abandoned his life of solitude and went to the Tabenna monastery so he could meet this holy woman the angel had proclaimed. When he arrived, he was allowed in (an unusual occurrence since typically men were not allowed inside a women's monastery, but because of his great holiness and his

---

27   Novakshonoff, *God's Fools*, 7.

old age he was welcomed). Once he entered, he asked that all the nuns be gathered together. Obediently, they all assembled before him—all except for Isidora. But Pitirim said that there must be others since he had not seen the woman "with a crown on her head." The sisters told him that they were all there, and that the only one absent was Isidora, who was in the kitchen. "But she is a fool," they said. Nonetheless, Pitirim asked them to bring her to him.

The sisters had to bring Isidora from the kitchen forcibly, but as she entered the room Pitirim could see with his spiritual sight that she was the one wearing not a rag but a splendid crown on her head. Pitirim fell prostrate at her feet and said, "Bless me, Amma!" In turn, Isidora fell at Pitirim's feet and asked instead for his blessing.

The sisters were shocked to see the famous and holy Pitirim behave in such a manner, and they said to him, "Father, do not let her deceive you. She is only a fool." "*You* are the fools," Pitirim replied. "She is mother of me and of you all. I pray that I might be found worthy of her on the Day of Judgment."

After Isidora received such honor and respect from so revered an ascetic as Pitirim, the sisters henceforth treated her with great deference. But this was not what Isidora desired. She wished to serve her Lord Christ in all humility, and thus she soon thereafter left the monastery to avoid any temptation to pride. Where she went and where she died no one knows, but it is certain that she prays for us all before the throne of God today. It is believed that she reposed around the year 365, and her memory is celebrated on May 10.

St. Isidore of Rostov
(fifteenth century)

I SIDORE WAS BORN IN WHAT is now called Brandenburg,
which at the time was a major city in Prussia. The area was pre-
dominantly Roman Catholic, and it is possible that he was brought
up in the Western faith. Whether he was born into Orthodoxy or was
received at a later age, he left Prussia for more Orthodox regions when
he was still a young man. His parents were quite rich, but Isidore dis-
tributed all his wealth to the poor before becoming a pilgrim and
wanderer. He traveled through many Orthodox lands before finally
coming to Rostov in Russia. He decided to stay there and practice the
difficult ascesis of being a fool for Christ. Playing the fool was entirely
voluntary for him.

Isidore constructed a small hut made of brush in a marshy area of Rostov and spent his nights there. The hut was in no wise weather-proof and did nothing to protect him from the elements, especially from the bitter winter weather, but Isidore dwelt there nonetheless.

During the day he would wander the streets of Rostov playing the fool and giving spiritual guidance to all who would listen. When he was tired, he would sometimes rest on a pile of trash or even on manure. In the evenings, he would return to his hut and spend most of the night standing in prayer, petitioning the Lord in particular on behalf of those who had caused him offense during the day. He also prayed earnestly for those to whom he'd given spiritual advice. He allowed himself only a little sleep each night.

As he wandered the streets and marketplace, Isidore would rarely enter anyone's home, and when he did he was more often than not thrown out. Once, though, when Prince Vladimir of Rostov was giving a dinner for the archbishop, Isidore went to his house early that day to ask for a drink of water from the prince's servant. (In reality, Isidore was not thirsty but instead wanted to give a blessing to Prince Vladimir's house.) The servant, however, not only refused to give him a cup of water but also drove him away.

During the dinner with the archbishop, the time came to serve the wine, and the servants found all the wine vessels empty. When they informed the prince of this embarrassing situation, he asked whether anyone else had been at the house that day. The servants said that only the mad beggar Isidore had been by earlier asking for a cup of water, but they did not let him into the house.

Remembering that the Lord had said, "Whoever gives a cup of cold water in My name will not lose his reward," Prince Vladimir hastened to send his servants out to find Isidore and bring him back to the house. Frantic searching did not prove profitable; Isidore was nowhere to be found. The prince was unsure what to do, as the dinner was nearly over and still they had served no wine.

Suddenly Isidore came into the house holding a prosphoron in his hand, which he presented to the archbishop, saying that he had just received it from the metropolitan in the church of St. Sophia in Kiev. As this was happening, the head servant noticed that all the wine vessels were now full of wine. He informed the prince, and everyone there was amazed at the miracle God had wrought through His servant Isidore.

On another occasion Isidore appeared at the wedding feast being held at Prince Simeon's house in honor of the prince's newly married friend Savva. Though the servants tried to drive Isidore away, he ignored them and made his way into the dining hall. He was carrying in his hand a small cap that he'd woven together out of grass and wildflowers. Making his way to the groom, he placed the cap on Savva's head and said, "Here! A Bishop's cap for you!"[28] Then Isidore quickly left and began playing with the children outside.

All present were bemused by the incident, believing it to be simply the jesting of a fool. It made no sense to the attendees, especially considering that Savva had just gotten married. But in the course of time, Savva's new wife died during childbirth, and he became so distraught with grief that he left the world and became a monk at the St. Therapont Monastery. There he was tonsured with the name Iosaph, and later he was ordained bishop of Rostov in 1481.

One miraculous event during Isidore's lifetime was not revealed until after his repose. It seems that a Rostov merchant was at sea with several of his comrades when the ship was overtaken by a violent storm. Fearing for their lives and remembering the account of

---

28   Sanidopoulos, "Saint Isidore of Rostov."

the prophet Jonah, the shipmates decided to cast lots to see whether there might be someone aboard causing their difficulties. The lot fell on the merchant (who also was the owner of the ship), and he was thrown overboard with only a wooden plank to save him.

Struggling to survive and nearing despair, the merchant suddenly saw someone walking on the water toward him. It was the Fool Isidore, and when he reached the merchant he held out his hand and asked him, "Do you recognize me?" The merchant replied in desperation, "The servant of God Isidor [sic]—help me . . ."[29]

Isidore pulled the man onto the plank which then, seemingly of its own accord, sped toward the ship that had sailed on safely. When the plank came aside the vessel, the merchant suddenly found himself back on the deck, surrounded by his awestruck comrades. They all glorified God for His mercy in delivering the merchant from death and restoring him to the ship, which was now out of danger.

After returning to Rostov, the merchant would prostrate himself before Isidore anytime he would see him. But Isidore had forbidden him from revealing to anyone what had happened and reminded him that he had been saved by God's grace and that Isidore had been only an intermediary. The merchant kept the event to himself until after the saint's death.

As Isidore neared the time of his repose, he remained in his hut for several days without going out to wander the streets but instead prayed hour after hour with tears. One morning an unusually wonderful fragrance was noticed throughout the city of Rostov, and the people searched for its source. They found that it was emanating from Isidore's hut, and inside they found the saint lying peacefully on the ground with his face toward heaven and his hands folded across his chest.

---

29 Novakshonoff, *God's Fools*, 101.

Saint Isidore has been called "an earthly angel and a heavenly man . . . a compassionate soul, and pure of thought, and vigilant heart and faith unassailed, and true love without pretense."[30]

Isidore was buried in his hut, and later a wooden chapel was built over his grave. In 1566, Tsar Ivan IV replaced the wooden chapel with a stone church, and in 1815 a silver shrine was placed on the grave, where numerous miracles have occurred.

---

30   "Venerable Isidore."

St. John of Ustyug
(† 1494)

—————————

LIKE ST. JOHN THE FORERUNNER, John of Ustyug was born to two elderly parents who had long prayed for a child. Also like his eponym, John demonstrated from his youth a desire to lead a godly life.

John practiced strict fasting even while still a child, eating nothing on Wednesdays and Fridays and only bread and water the rest of the week. When his mother asked him why he observed so strict a fasting rule, he replied that he wanted to avoid feeding his flesh so that it would not become his enemy and tempt him from following Christ.

At some point in his early life, the family moved from Ustyug to Orlets, but shortly thereafter John's father died. His mother then entered the Holy Trinity Convent, where the young John was allowed to live with her the rest of his childhood. While there, John continued his strict fasting rule and began practicing the discipline of silence. Seeing his unusual devotion, his mother left him to God's will to do as he saw fit in his struggle.

After gaining his majority, John returned to Ustyug and took up residence in a small hut that a devout friend had built for him next to the Dormition Church. It was after his return to Ustyug that John increased his struggles and took up the difficult challenge of becoming a fool for Christ. He began wandering the streets of Ustyug during the day wearing only a long shirt that was tied about his waist with a rope and, when tired, would rest on heaps of manure about town. He allowed himself to become the object of much derision and abuse by the townsfolk, but at night he would frequently remain awake all night in prayer, praying especially for those who had abused him during the day.

We only know about his ardent nocturnal prayer life because a priest was curious about what John did during the night. One Fr. Gregory of the cathedral church decided one night to creep up to John's hut and peek through a crack in the wall to investigate. He observed John praying for hours while standing and holding his hands aloft, and then after an exhausting period of prayer he saw John stir the coals of his fire, cross himself, and pray, "Let the light of Your countenance shine upon us, O Lord!"[31] Then he lay down on the glowing coals.

Horrified by this, Fr. Gregory burst into the hut to rescue John from certain injury. But when John saw Fr. Gregory, he simply got up off the coals unharmed and warned him sternly not to tell anyone of what he had seen until after his death.

Although he became known throughout Ustyug for having been given the gift of wonderworking, only one other incident is recorded

---

31   Novakshonoff, *God's Fools*, 96.

from his life. Once when Princess Maria, the wife of the governor Prince Theodore Krasny, became seriously ill the prince sent a servant to find the Fool John to ask him to pray for Maria. When the servant finally found him, John was lying on a pile of manure and called out to the servant, "And how is the good Prince Theodore and his princess?"[32] before even being presented with the prince's request. When the servant returned home, he found the princess well.

John reposed on May 29, 1494, and he was buried next to the church by which he had lived all his adult life. Later the Church of the All-Honorable Cross was built over his grave.

---

32   Novakshonoff, 97.

St. Lyubov of Ryazan
(1852-1921)

L YUBOV WAS BORN IN THE city of Pronsk, Ryazan region, on August 28, 1852, to two very poor but devout parents, Maria and Semeon Sukhanovsky. She was baptized in the Church of St. Nicholas by Fr. Pyotr Pavlov, the father of the famous scientist Ivan Pavlov. Her own father died not long after her younger sister Olga was born, and her mother was left with only the two daughters since two sons had died earlier. Without Semeon's financial support, they were among the poorest families in all of Ryazan. The house in which they eventually settled in Lyubov's childhood was also the house in which she lived the rest of her life, dying there in 1921.

As if losing her two sons and husband were not trial enough, more sorrow bore on Maria's heart because Lyubov was an invalid, unable to walk or even stand. Though bedridden, she was a cheerful child who, by her sanguine countenance, brought light into her poor mother's life. Maria taught Lyubov how to pray and to read and write, and the young girl delighted in prayer and in reading spiritual books. She especially loved praying before the icon of St. Nicholas.

One day when she was fifteen and alone in the house, St. Nicholas appeared to her and told her to rise and walk and become a fool for Christ. Miraculously, Lyubov got up out of bed and stood on her own. When her mother returned home, she was ecstatic to see her crippled daughter standing, completely healed of her long infirmity. Lyubov told her mother everything that had happened, and Maria went to consult the family's priest regarding the matter. He advised that they allow Lyubov to do as the saint requested.

Able now to walk, Lyubov began praying in all the churches in Ryazan and even visited the Kazan Monastery for women where she stayed for a time, receiving spiritual instruction. Desiring to become an ascetic, she decided to return home and make a niche between the stove and the wall in her house her "cell." There she remained as a recluse for three years, engaging the whole time in intense prayer. At the end of three years, she went back into the world once more to be among people and take up the difficult podvig of becoming a fool for Christ as St. Nicholas had directed.

Though back in the world, Lyubov never ceased from praying for all those around her, and she resumed going to churches and monasteries throughout Ryazan to pray. She cared greatly for all people and was known for her generosity and kindheartedness. For her deep devotion to Christ, the Lord blessed her with the gifts of clairvoyance and foresight, which allowed her to be of even greater help to those in need.

One unusual thing Lyubov did was to go into shops in Ryazan and gather items to give to the needy. She always knew exactly what each recipient would need, and she would collect only what was necessary.

She never paid for these items, nor did she ever keep anything for herself, but the merchants did not mind—instead, they felt blessed by Lyubov's presence in their stores.

Since Lyubov herself was among the poorest in Ryazan, people sometimes would give her things to help meet her needs, be it food or clothing or other helpful items. She would accept these gifts with deep gratitude, but within hours she would give them away to someone more needy. On occasion she would refuse a gift, saying that the person offering the gift needed it more.

Being of a cheerful nature, Lyubov's apparel reflected her buoyant spirit. She always dressed plainly but in bright colors. Her favorite color was pink, and she frequently would be seen wearing a pink scarf on her head.

Perhaps her most memorable characteristic was the way in which she often revealed her insights to others. Frequently, instead of using words, she would use visual means to communicate, especially by taking paper and scissors and cutting out images that would represent what she wished to declare—a kind of Lyubovian kirigami. For instance, if she knew someone was about to embark on a journey she might cut out a horse or carriage; if she foresaw someone marrying, she would cut out crowns; if she presaged a person's death, she would cut out a coffin. Once, when approached by a young woman who asked her whether or not she should become a nun, in reply Lyubov took paper and scissors and cut out an entire monastery in great detail, including even the fence, church, and choir. Thus she answered the question, and in fact the young woman became a nun and sang in the monastery choir, as she possessed one of the rarest of voices—a female bass.

At other times Lyubov would use other visual means. She once encountered two young girls and gave each an icon, one an icon of St. Alexander Nevsky and the other an icon of St. Anna of Kashin. When the girls grew up, the first girl married a man named Alexander and lived near the Alexander Nevsky train station; the second, just like St. Anna, became a widow with two small children.

On another occasion Lyubov visited a family just as the grandmother of the house was serving tea, and she came in carrying a piece of cloth in her hand. When asked what she was holding, she said that on her way there she passed by a funeral parlor where they were upholstering a coffin with some lovely velvet. She brought a piece of the velvet and handed it to the grandmother, telling her to take it. No one understood what this odd presentation meant, but moments later word arrived that the grandmother's godmother had just passed away. This was Lyubov's way of preparing the grandmother for the news.

Shortly before Tsar Nicholas II abdicated in 1917, Lyubov was observed running excitedly through the streets shouting, "The walls of Jericho are falling, the walls of Jericho are falling[!]"[33] No one knew what she meant by this, but soon with the abdication of the tsar and the ensuing revolution, it all became clear that the blessed one had foreseen the troubles ahead. She continued to comfort and console people during the time of the Russian Revolution and would inform them of future tragedies in advance so that they might better prepare. She foresaw the closing of the Kazan Monastery long before anyone thought such an event was even possible, and she revealed to several of the nuns what their futures would be after the closing of the monastery. All of her predictions came to pass exactly as she had foretold.

Three weeks before her death, Lyubov informed a friend that she was about to die and asked that her coffin be lined with pink cloth, her favorite color. The friend found this last request a difficult one because of all the troubles of the time: stores were empty, and even if any fabric was available it only could be bought with coupons, which the family did not have. Out of desperation she decided just to line

---

33 "Blessed Liubov."

the plain wooden coffin with gauze. She went to a pharmacy to purchase it, and all they had was pink gauze! There was enough to line and adorn the coffin as Lyubov had requested, all in pink.

Great throngs turned out to accompany the saint to her grave, as she was much beloved by all of Ryazan. A deacon of Ryazan erected a monument over her grave, but in time, as the force of atheism ensued, the blessed one was forgotten and her grave grew untended. As church after church throughout Russia was closed or destroyed by the communist government, there came a time when only a single parish remained in Ryazan, and no one visited the saint's grave anymore. But one day a soldier appeared at the cemetery and asked where the grave of Lyubov Sukhanovskaya could be found. When he located it, he put up a cross and installed a metal fence around the grave. When asked why he did this, he explained that he had been deathly ill and the doctors could do nothing for him. Then one night Lyubov appeared to him in a dream and told him not to be discouraged but to go to Ryazan and find her grave and enclose it with a fence. If he would do this, she said, he would be healthy and happy. After performing this beneficence, he indeed found himself free of his illness, and in gratitude he visited her grave and had a panikhida served for Lyubov every year.

Many other miracles have been performed through the blessed one, and in 1987 she was recognized as a saint. Since pink was the saint's favorite color, in 1992 a pink chapel was erected over her grave. In June 1998 her holy relics were transferred to the St. Nicholas-Yamskoy temple in Ryazan.

St. Maria of Diveyevo
(† 1931)

T HE YEAR OF MARIA'S BIRTH is unknown, but she is known
to have been born into a peasant family in Goletkov, Tambov
Province. Though her father's name was Zakhar, Maria always preferred the patronymic Ivanovna rather than Zakharovna because, as
she once said later in life, "All of us blessed ones are Ivanovnas [i.e.,
daughters of John], after St. John the Forerunner."[34]

Maria's mother died when she was thirteen and her father a year
later, so that she was orphaned by age fourteen. At first she was taken
in by her eldest brother's family, but the sister-in-law did not like her
and made her life very difficult. This was partly because Maria had

---

34   Sanidopoulos, "Saint Maria Ivanovna of Diveyevo."

been "different" from early childhood, very much a loner who did not play with other children but preferred going to church and never engaging in community frivolities. She also preferred dressing in worn-out clothes and tended toward being unkempt in appearance.

She is said to have received visions of St. Seraphim of Sarov and of the Diveyevo Monastery from her youth, although she had not yet been to the monastery. When a group of women and girls from the village decided to go on a pilgrimage to Sarov, Maria elected to join them. Because of her unenviable home life and the visions she had received, she chose not to return to the village at the end of the pilgrimage but instead wandered the forests between Diveyevo's surrounding communities. Having nothing but the shabby clothing she had worn on the journey, she soon wandered about half naked and was often mocked and mistreated by local peasants who thought her mad.

During this period of wandering, her only place of semi-permanence was the Diveyevo Monastery, which she would visit on many occasions. Whenever she would arrive there, she would be covered in ticks and sores, and her clothing would be thoroughly worn and often laden with mud. Some in the convent saw in her a divine presence and would care for her and provide her with clean clothing; but when she would next return, she would be in the same condition as before, even having been bitten by dogs or beaten by cruel peasants. Others in the convent saw her only as a troublesome guest who was beyond help, and they would even call the local police to come and take her away. But the police thought her only a simpleton and would let her go.

Despite all the tragedies, hardships, and persecutions she faced, no one ever heard Maria complain or bewail her state. God was her solace and comfort, and He graced her with a special intuition. People began to notice her great humility and godliness and often would seek her out for counsel and guidance.

One of the nuns at Diveyevo who saw the virtue of Maria's life was Paraskeva Ivanovna. As Paraskeva neared the end of her life, she prophesied about Maria: "I am still alive and sitting at the loom, but another is already walking about. Soon she will sit where I am."[35] By this she indicated that after her own repose, Maria would cease her forest wanderings and would take up permanent residence in Diveyevo.

This happened just as she had foretold. But when Maria came to the church at Diveyevo for Paraskeva's funeral, her odd behavior troubled some of the nuns so that they cast her out with instructions never to return. As Paraskeva's coffin was being carried into the church, a peasant in attendance came to the nuns and said, "What a slave of God you have banished from your monastery; she just told me my whole life and all of my sins. Take her back into the monastery, or you will lose her forever." And so the nuns ran after her and brought her back to her new home.

God blessed Maria with the gifts of healing and clairvoyance, but in order not to bring glory to herself she would try to conceal these blessings by speaking foolishly and sometimes cursing. She could be a chatterbox, speaking fast and frequently, and would sprinkle her speech with colorful words that often offended the nuns and those who came to visit her. She did this so that others would not think more highly of her than they ought.

Maria received a steady stream of people during the trying time of the Russian Revolution, many coming to her for physical healing and many more for spiritual counseling and prayer. She healed one woman of a disease of the eye by anointing her with oil from a lampada, as

---

35 All other quotations in this chapter come from "Blessed Maria Ivanovna of Diveyevo."

she also healed in the same manner a nun who suffered from severe eczema and had received no benefit from numerous physicians.

Her gift of clairvoyance was also well attested. One day a young boy came to see her and she said, "Well, the priest Alexis has arrived!" In the course of time, the young boy grew up to become a hieromonk at Sarov.

One July night in 1918 Maria became exceedingly agitated and paced about her room weeping and crying out, "The tsarevnas! By bayonets! Oh, the bayonets!" The others did not know what to make of this until news arrived much later that the royal family had been martyred by the Bolsheviks in Yekaterinburg—on the same night as her outburst.

As civil strife continued to escalate in Russia, the nuns asked Maria how much longer they at Diveyevo could continue to live peacefully. Maria calmly replied, "Three months." And in exactly three months from that date the authorities asked everyone to leave the monastery. Diveyevo Monastery was closed in 1927, and Maria had already foreseen much of what lay ahead for her country. She foresaw the concentration camps and years of godlessness that were to come. To help her sisters prepare for the imminent trials, she encouraged them in their faith and even foretold an eventual rebirth of the Diveyevo monastery. She said that several of them would still be in a convent, "Only instead of your names, you will all have numbers"—foretelling their time in concentration camps. Some sisters kept bemoaning the fact that there was no longer a monastery and never would be again, but Maria would become insistent and shout, "There will be! Yes, there will be!" and would bang her fist forcefully on the table for emphasis.

Once the inhabitants had been ordered out of the monastery, Maria lived temporarily with caring believers in several different villages surrounding Diveyevo. At one point she was even arrested by the communist authorities, but after interrogating her they released her, believing that she was insane. In 1930 Maria moved to the village of Cherevatovo where she reposed after much suffering on August 26, 1931. Maria was glorified in 2004.

St. Michael of Klops Monastery (fifteenth century)

T HE LIVES OF MOST FOOLS for Christ tend to be somewhat
mysterious, but that of St. Michael is exceptionally enigmatic.

As Matins was being served in the Klops Monastery on June 23,
1408, Hieromonk Macarius censed the church and the nearby cells,
which included his own. As he approached his cell, he noticed that the
door was open, and inside at his desk sat a man dressed as a monastic,
busily copying the Acts of the Apostles. Not recognizing the man, Fr.
Macarius hastened to tell the abbot and the other brethren about this
mysterious guest. When they came to the cell, the stranger was still sitting calmly, copying from the Scriptures. When they asked who he was,
they were answered only with the same question. The brothers assumed
the man to be a simpleminded fool who somehow had managed to

sneak into the monastery and unlock Fr. Macarius's cell door—though they never learned how he had accomplished either task.

Though perceived as a fool, the stranger was able to chant and read eloquently during the Divine Liturgy and from the lives of the saints during meals. He was given a cell and participated in the life and worship of the monastery, but every attempt to learn who he was or where he came from was unsuccessful. He was strict in fasting and prayer, and he kept nothing in his cell whatever—not even a mat for sleeping. Observing his virtuous behavior, the monks honored him as a very holy individual; but in order not to allow this honor to lead to pride, the stranger adopted foolish behavior in everything he did.

It wasn't until the famous Prince Constantine Dmitrievich visited the monastery that the monks learned the identity of their holy fool. They asked the stranger to read from the book of Job during meal-time, and Prince Constantine seemed to recognize his voice. Coming closer to examine the unknown reader, the prince suddenly bowed to the stranger and announced that he was none other than his own kinsman, Michael Maximovich.

When asked why he had not earlier revealed his identity, Michael replied, "Only the Creator knows me, and who I am."[36] Once they learned of his noble blood, the monks began to show greater honor to Michael, but this was something he wished to avoid. Thus he began increasing his struggles in foolishness, setting a great example to his brethren in all monastic work, vigils, and prayer. For this he received from God the gift of clairvoyance.

There are many accounts of his prophetic gift. One time, when Prince Constantine came again to visit the monastery, he asked Michael to pray for him because his brothers had deprived him of his rightful inheritance. Though distraught over this, the prince remained charitable, and Michael told him to build a church in the name of the

---

36 "Venerable Michael the Fool-for-Christ of the Klops Monastery, Novgorod."

Holy Trinity. By doing this, he said, the prince would receive not only a heavenly home but also would be reconciled with his brothers. On the very day that the church was consecrated, the prince told the abbot that he had been restored to his patrimony, just as Michael had foretold.

Another time, a great drought occurred in the regions around Novgorod so that even the river that supplied water to the monastery went dry. As the monks went out in search of water, someone saw Michael writing in the sand next to the riverbed. When the abbot heard of this, he went out to see what had been written and found the words, "I will take the cup of salvation [Ps. 116:13], let the well-spring show forth on this spot."[37] When the abbot asked him what the words meant, Michael would only repeat the same words back to him. But when they dug in the dry earth where Michael had written the words, a spring of water came forth with enough water to sustain the monastery and the people living near it.

Later, there was a famine in the region, and the people came to the monastery to beg for bread. Michael gave bread to all who came, to the point that the abbot began to be concerned that the supply of bread would be utterly depleted. But Michael told him, "If five thousand, not counting women and children, were fed with five loaves . . . are we to spurn our supplicants?"[38] He encouraged the abbot to feed all who came and to trust God. The abbot did so, and for the duration of the famine the supply of bread in the storehouses never diminished, despite how many loaves they gave away.

Once during the Divine Liturgy Michael told the abbot that there were guests outside who wished to come to them. As they were leaving the service they saw three strangers in the courtyard, and Michael invited them in to eat with them. Once inside, one of the guests said that they had other companions outside the monastery, and when

---

37   "Venerable Michael the Fool-for-Christ of the Klops Monastery, Novgorod."
38   Novakshonoff, *God's Fools*, 86.

the gates were opened to invite them in as well, thirty armed robbers rushed in, intending to rob and vandalize the monastery after first eating with the monks. Two of the thirty kept watch, and Michael said to them, "Why don't you eat? You may be certain that your evil intentions will not be fulfilled."[39]

At that, the two clasped their chests and collapsed onto the floor, unable even to utter a word. The other robbers were terrified by this, and they fled in haste, even giving gifts to the abbot and asking him to pray for and minister to the two afflicted souls as they left. After a short time, the two thieves recovered. One left the monastery promising never to engage in thievery again, and the other stayed and himself became a monk, repenting fully of his past ways. At first the abbot was reluctant to tonsure him, fearful that he might resume his evil ways and harm the monastery; but Michael advised him to accept the former thief because he would become a true monk but would not be with them long. The repentant thief did in fact become a monk, but he died about two years later.

One day in 1440 Michael, while visiting the Vyashersky-Nikolai Monastery, went into the belfry and began ringing the bells wildly. When asked what this was all about, Michael said in a foolish manner, "[T]here is a joy in Moscow! There has been born to the Grand Prince a son . . . Ivan. And what a son! He will be heir to all the Russian Tsardom and will be terrible to all the neighboring countries. He will submit you to his will; he will destroy all your self-will."[40] Indeed, on January 22, 1440, Prince Ivan Vasilievich (later to be known as Ivan Grozny or Ivan the Terrible) was born. He conquered Novgorod in November 1471 and was the first to unite the Russian people under one tsar.

Despite being known for his great devotion, Michael nevertheless bore the scorn of many because of his foolishness. Once a group of

---

39   Novakshonoff, 87.
40   Novakshonoff, 88.

children taunted him by calling him names and throwing rocks and refuse at him. Michael ignored the taunts, but he walked up to a boy standing nearby and took him by the hair. He then told him that he should study books with great diligence because he was to become the archbishop of Novgorod. The boy did indeed become a scholar, and later he became a priest, then a bishop, and eventually was elevated to the archbishopric as the great and renowned hierarch Jonah.

After living in the Klops Monastery for more than forty-six years, Michael suddenly stopped appearing in church for Divine Liturgy and instead could be found sitting on the ground just outside the church. When the abbot asked why he would not come in to the Liturgy, Michael simply quoted Psalm 132:14, "This is My resting place forever; / Here I will dwell, for I have desired it."

As the Nativity fast commenced, Michael fell into a deep illness which kept him bedridden into January. On January 10 he called all the brothers to him to ask their forgiveness and to bid them farewell. He also promised that he would not leave the monastery even after his death. The next day he miraculously rose from his bed and attended the Divine Liturgy, and afterward even took coal and incense and lit a censer to take back to his cell. The abbot, encouraged by Michael's renewed strength, sent food to him so that he could recover more fully. But when the brothers arrived at his cell with the food, they found him lying still with his hands across his chest in eternal repose. The monastery was then filled with the fragrance of incense, and all the monks mourned tearfully.

Because it was deep winter, the ground where they had intended to bury the saint was frozen solid and a grave could not be dug. Suddenly the abbot remembered the spot near the church where Michael had been sitting during the Liturgies, and he ordered that they try digging a grave there. To everyone's surprise the ground at that spot was as soft as during summer, and so he was laid to rest where he had foretold.

St. Nicholai of Vologda
(1777-1837)

ST. NICHOLAI WAS BORN NICHOLAI Matveevich Rynin on May 22, 1777, in Vologda, Russia. Born into a wealthy merchant family, Nicholai was taught to read and write by his parents and from his youth desired to serve God and his fellow man. As he reached the age of majority, he rejected wealth and gave away his portion of his inheritance to the poor. He went around Vologda dressed as a beggar and lived off charity.

Nicholai spent his days attending services at various churches throughout the city, and at night he spent his time in solitude and prayer, generally in some place where no one could find him.

Later he began to roam from city to city, spending time not only in Vologda but also in Kadnikov and Totma. He is remembered for always wearing a blue canvas *balakhon* (a kind of loose overall), a long white shirt, and leather straps on his legs. He almost always carried a large staff as he walked and would go hatless in both winter and summer, though sometimes he would tie a towel around his head in bitter cold.

Nicholai's voice was said to be very husky, gravelly, and even garbled, but like the prophets of old, his speech typically carried special meaning, the significance of which would sometimes not be revealed until later. As a visionary, he foresaw and predicted the cholera epidemic that swept through Vologda a week before it began, as well as many other events that the archimandrite validated as being correct.

Nicholai carried with him various things he would give to those whom he encountered, always providing items of special significance for their particular situation. To a hungry person he would give food, to someone experiencing grief he might give coal, to others bread, and for the children always sweets. He was a great friend to children and was much loved by them. Christ said, "unless you are converted and become as little children, you will by no means enter the kingdom of heaven" (Matt. 18:3), and Nicholai maintained the heart of a child throughout his life. Though he could be strict in his counsel to adults who practiced unrighteousness, he was very kind to all children and they generally followed him about with purity of heart.

One time Nicholai was a guest in the home of a nobleman of the city, one Lord Onisifor. Suddenly Nicholai told his host that he knew he had sixteen cassocks in his closet and that Onisifor was to give one to him immediately. Unsure why Nicholai would be in need of a cassock, Lord Onisifor nevertheless gave him one, and Nicholai then hastened outside. In the courtyard he met a man who was dressed in rags and was on his way to petition the lord for help in finding shelter. Nicholai gave him the cassock, seemingly knowing ahead of time what was needed when he had asked the lord for one of his.

The blessed Nicholai died on March 19, 1837, at the age of fifty-nine. He was buried in the Bogorodskoye Cemetery in Vologda. Beloved by the people of Vologda to this very day, there is now a cathedral there in his memory where many healings and other miracles have taken place, as recorded in a journal kept in the cathedral. Nicholai was glorified in 1988, and the chapel over his grave was restored and consecrated the same year.

St. Nicholas of Novgorod
(† 1392)

L IKE A NUMBER OF OTHER fools for Christ who abandoned all worldly goods and honor, Nicholas was born into a wealthy and distinguished family of Novgorod. From his earliest days, he was noted for being exceptionally devoted to Christ, attending services regularly, and with great joy and eagerness embracing fasting and prayer. As others observed his inestimable piety, he began receiving praise and commendations from his fellow citizens. He did not desire this because he wanted all praise to go to God, not to himself, and he saw such adulation as a gateway to pride and downfall.

To avoid temptation to vainglory, Nicholas turned to the challenging practice of foolishness for the Lord's sake. Though of wealthy estate, he began wandering the city dressed in rags, even in the bitterly cold winters. The citizens of Novgorod perceived him as a beggar and vagrant and often subjected him to mockery, insults, and even beatings. All these he bore with patience and forgiveness in his heart, and he considered it a blessing to be persecuted for the Lord's sake.

During the time Nicholas lived in Novgorod, the city was divided in strife between two quadrants: the Torgov quarter and the Sophia quarter. For some reason there was great rivalry between these two parts of Novgorod, and the populace engaged in trifling disputes and quarreling. As it happened, there was another fool for Christ in Novgorod contemporary with Nicholas, a man named Theodore. In order to demonstrate to the people of Novgorod the absurdity of the endless squabbles with which they antagonized one another, Nicholas and Theodore feigned being mortal enemies who could not be reconciled. In one such demonstration, Nicholas and Theodore yelled at each other across the Volkhov River, one on each side, and eventually Nicholas walked across the river as if on dry land and threw a head of cabbage at Theodore. After that, Nicholas was nicknamed *Kochanov*, which means "cabbage head," and in many catalogs of saints he can be found listed as Nicholas Kochanov of Novgorod.

Once when Nicholas had been invited to a feast, the servants at the feast turned him away, thinking he was a beggar because of his shabby clothing. Nicholas did not protest but left peacefully and without argument. However, on his departure all the wine at the feast disappeared, and it wasn't until the host sent servants to bring him back to the feast and pray for them that it reappeared.

Saint Nicholas reposed in the Lord in 1392, and his relics now rest beneath a crypt in the church of the Great Martyr Panteleimon, which was built over his grave.

IVANUSHKO
IVANUSHKO!
·EAT·OUR·
BREAD·
&·OUR·SALT
·NOT·
·CHRISTIAN·
BLOOD!

St. Nicholas of Pskov
(† 1576)

V ERY LITTLE IS KNOWN ABOUT the life of St. Nicholas of Pskov beyond his famous encounter with Tsar Ivan IV (Ivan Grozny or Ivan the Terrible), related below. He is believed to have been a lifelong resident of Pskov and a well-known fool for Christ throughout the region and perhaps most of Russia.

The greatest amount of information we have about Nicholas involves a single day in his life, February 20, 1570. On this day, the second Sunday of Great Lent, the city of Pskov trembled because of the expected visit of Tsar Ivan IV and his army. Ivan had recently completed his campaign against the city of Novgorod, where he directed his soldiers to massacre thousands of its citizens. This was one of the most brutal and notorious acts ever perpetrated by a Russian tsar against his own people.

The entire population of Pskov feared that his wrath had not been quenched by the bloodshed in Novgorod and would be visited upon their own city. In anticipation of the tsar's arrival, the citizenry prepared a profusion of welcoming gifts of bread and salt (the traditional means of cordial invitation in Russia), but despite their attempts to appease the tsar's acrimony they remained in dread of his arrival.

When presented with the gifts of bread and salt on his approach to the city gates, Ivan reportedly brushed them aside in disdain, causing the crowds to fear him all the more. As they hastily prostrated themselves before the tsar, from out of the crowd came Nicholas the Fool riding a children's stick horse and shouting, "Ivanushko, Ivanushko [meaning "Little Ivan"], eat our bread and salt, and not Christian blood."[41] Infuriated at this, the tsar ordered Nicholas to be seized, but a strong gust of wind suddenly blew up the snow in great swirls, making Nicholas invisible to the guards and he escaped.

Since it was Sunday, Ivan's procession went to the cathedral in Pskov, and the tsar himself entered and stood for an entire moleben given for his health. As he was leaving the cathedral, Nicholas again approached him and invited him to come to his cell beneath the bell tower for refreshment. The fact that the tsar consented to do so gives credence to the belief that Nicholas was already well-known as a devout fool for Christ.

Upon entering the cramped cell, the tsar noticed that a slab of raw meat lay on the table. Nicholas said to him, "Eat, Little Ivan, eat!" But Ivan, annoyed and insulted, replied that he was a Christian and did not eat meat during Lent.

---

41   Underwood, "The Prophetic Voice."

Nicholas then said, "Does Ivashka [another diminutive for Ivan] think that eating a piece of animal meat during a fast is a sin, whereas eating as much human meat as he has already eaten is no sin?"[42]

Furious at receiving such a rebuke, Ivan stormed from the cell, evidently intent on repeating the evils he had visited upon Novgorod. Nicholas ran after him, giving him a stern warning: "Do not dare touch us, you vagabond! Leave us quickly, because if you dally you will have nothing on which to flee from here."

Ignoring the saint, Ivan ordered his army to proceed with his commands. But again Nicholas cried out, "If your warriors touch a single hair on the least child in this city, a fire from heaven will overtake you. God's judgment is already hanging over you, and you will not escape death by fire from heaven."

At that moment bolts of lightning shot from the roiling storm clouds that had been gathering above the city, terrifying even Tsar Ivan's most courageous soldiers. Word came to Ivan that one of the bolts had struck the tsar's own horse, killing it instantly. This caused Ivan to recall the words Nicholas had spoken, that if he did not leave quickly he would have nothing on which to flee. Terrified, he turned to the clergy, asked them to pray for him, then took the horse of one of his servants and fled in haste. Thus the city of Pskov was saved from destruction, despite Ivan's initial plan.

Aside from this one event, however, we know almost nothing else about Nicholas's life. He is known to have reposed in the Lord February 28, 1576, and initially to have been buried in a crypt beneath Holy Trinity Cathedral—a site granted only to the most revered individuals, thus once more attesting to the saint's wide acclaim. His remains were later transferred to the right chapel of the cathedral.

---

42   Manaev, "Why Did Russian Tsars Love 'Holy Fools'?"

Nicholas is known to have helped save Pskov a second time, after his repose. When the invading Polish army threatened the city in 1581, St. Nicholas and St. Cornell (the former abbot of the Pskov Caves Monastery and a contemporary of St. Nicholas) appeared to many Pskov citizens in a dream. In the vision, the two were standing with the Theotokos and asking her to intercede with Christ for the people of Pskov. The Theotokos fulfilled their request, and Christ again delivered the city from destruction.

St. Paraskeva of Diveyevo
(1795-1915)

BORN TO A FAMILY OF serfs in 1795 in the village of
Nikolskoye, Tambov, and originally christened Irina Ivanovna,
Paraskeva was given in marriage to a man named Feodor when she
was seventeen years old. By all accounts she was a dutiful wife with
a meek bearing who was dedicated to her husband and to prayer. She
did not participate in community activities beyond church, but she
was much admired, particularly by her parents-in-law.

Irina and Feodor were not blessed with children. After fifteen
years of serving their Russian masters as serfs, Feodor and Irina were
sold to a German family named Schmidt. Five years after that, however, Feodor contracted tuberculosis and died. The Schmidts initially
tried to convince Irina to remarry, but she adamantly refused.

Sometime later, the Schmidts found that two valuable paintings were missing from their household, and one of the servant women accused Irina of being the thief. The police arrested her and proceeded to beat her severely, but Irina consistently pleaded innocence in the matter. When her masters consulted a fortune teller to help them solve the mystery, the fortune teller said that the paintings had indeed been stolen by a woman named Irina, but not by the Irina who had been arrested.

With that, Irina was released and returned to the Schmidt household, but she was never thereafter comfortable living with her heterodox masters. Thus she ran away and went to Kiev on a pilgrimage. During this pilgrimage, she knew she was being called to devote herself entirely to Christ, and after having been unfairly punished herself, she felt that she could identify more with Christ's own sufferings at the hands of evil accusers.

After several months, the police found the runaway serf in Kiev and returned her forcefully to her masters. The Schmidts felt guilty over her earlier mistreatment and pardoned her from running away. They reinstated her in their household, allowing her to serve as their gardener. But having once tasted the beauty of the holy places of Kiev, Irina fled once again in an attempt to assume a spiritual life.

Once more, however, the Schmidts sent search parties for her, and yet again she was apprehended by the police in Kiev and returned to her masters. By this time, the Schmidts' patience with her had reached an end, and they unceremoniously threw her out into the street with nothing but the clothes she was wearing.

This action pleased Irina, since during her last visit to Kiev she had received tonsure with the name Paraskeva, and she saw her expulsion as a sign that God was calling her to the difficult path of a fool for Christ. For the next five years she wandered about the streets, acting the fool and becoming an object of ridicule throughout the village. She lived outside throughout all seasons, and eventually she removed herself even further from the world by hiding in the Sarov forest. Here she lived for roughly twenty years in a small cave that she had dug out with her own hands.

Though as a young wife she was said to have had a very pleasant appearance, after years in the forest Paraskeva began to resemble St. Mary of Egypt, becoming exceedingly thin, brown-skinned from the sun, and she had short hair. She wore no shoes and only a man's monastic shirt, and sometimes a worn overcoat that was open at the chest. Knowledge of her spread among the people (as often happened with holy souls who would withdraw from the world—people still learned of them and sought them out), and people began to come to her for spiritual advice and for prayers.

Paraskeva experienced some of the same suffering as St. Seraphim of Sarov, whom she revered. Once a band of Tartars robbed a local church, and when Paraskeva encountered them in the forest she chastised them for their evil deed. They in turn beat her and left her for dead with a broken skull. When the Tartars bragged about this encounter to a peasant in Sarov, the peasant perceived that it must be Paraskeva they were talking about, and so he went out and rescued her. In time she recovered from her wounds, but just as St. Seraphim was left bent over after robbers once broke his back, Paraskeva's skull healed unevenly and her head perpetually leaned to one side.

During her time in the forest, Paraskeva would visit the Diveyevo Monastery on occasion, staying sometimes for weeks or months at a time. She visited especially the Fool for Christ Pelagia Ivanovna, who had known and was blessed by St. Seraphim of Sarov. Often Paraskeva would come to the monastery carrying little dolls with her, which she would call her "children." She finally moved into the monastery permanently a year before Pelagia's repose.

Paraskeva kept a strict rule of prayer, always rising at midnight to pray and insisting that anyone living with her do the same. She also would spend much of her time knitting socks or spinning thread, reciting the Jesus Prayer endlessly as she worked. When a visitor once asked her if she might join Paraskeva at the monastery, she replied, "Well, why not? Come to us in Sarov, we'll collect mushrooms and knit stockings"[43]—meaning by this that they would do prostrations and say the Jesus Prayer together.

Paraskeva knew many prayers from memory, but she also often prayed straight from the heart. She was intimate with the Theotokos and called the Mother of God "Mamenka [Mommy] behind the glass."[44] She never really ceased from prayer and frequently could be observed stopping even while working in the field and prostrating herself in prayer.

Curious to know exactly how Paraskeva did her midnight prayers, one of the nuns who would see her light candles in her cell every midnight decided one night to observe her surreptitiously through the window. As she stealthily approached one of the windows, however, Paraskeva suddenly pulled shut the curtains (which were never closed). The nun then sneaked to another window, only to have the same thing happen. This occurred at each window she approached until all the curtains were shut.

On another occasion a nun was with Paraskeva when she began to pray and—once more like St. Mary of Egypt—she was observed to rise in the air, her feet no longer touching the ground as she prayed.

When the time came for Seraphim of Sarov to be glorified (1903), pilgrims of all ranks gathered for the event, including even Tsar Nicholas II and his family. The tsar had heard about Paraskeva and arranged to meet with her privately while he was at Diveyevo. Paraskeva had the habit of serving her guests tea, and when she foresaw anything bad happening to them in the future she would add extra sugar to the tea. It is said that when Tsar Nicholas visited her,

---

43   Orlovsky, "Blessed Prascovia (Parasceva) Ivanovna of Sarov and Diveyevo."
44   Orlovsky.

she poured so much sugar into his tea that it overflowed the cup. She foretold not only the birth of the heir (Alexis had not yet been born in 1903) but also the fall of the monarchy. Nicholas, for his part, referred to Paraskeva as a great servant of God, and he was especially impressed with her honest heart: she treated Nicholas like any other human and not as royalty.

Paraskeva kept a portrait of the tsar in her room and sometimes would be seen making prostrations before it. When asked why she would make prostrations to the tsar, she would reply, "Sillies! He will be higher than all the tsars!"[45]—foretelling his martyrdom and glorification.

Paraskeva became paralyzed not long before her death and suffered a great deal. A nun from St. Petersburg related that she witnessed Paraskeva's soul rising up to the heavens on the night she died. She reposed on September 22, 1915, at 120 years of age.

---

45   Orlovsky.

St. Pelagia of Diveyevo
(1809-1884)

PELAGIA IVANOVNA SEREBRENNIKOVA WAS BORN into a wealthy merchant family in Arzamas in the year 1809. Her father died while she was still a child, and sometime after she fell into a serious illness that kept her bedridden for an extensive period. When she recovered, it was said she was a very different child from what she had been before and often acted bizarrely in public. This caused those around her to nickname her "Fool" even in childhood. Her stepfather often would punish her severely for such behavior, and it was many years later that her mother finally realized she had been gifted with the grace to become a fool for Christ.

When she was nineteen, her mother and stepfather gave her away in marriage to a man named Sergei, but her odd behavior continued.

She often would go barefoot and scantily clad as she ran around the streets in seeming madness and then pray all night in front of the doors of the church. For these behaviors her husband would sometimes beat her and even restrain her with chains. Such were the customary punishments of the day.

But her husband and mother both were very concerned about her well-being, and so they decided to take her to see St. Seraphim of Sarov to ask for his aid. Saint Seraphim took her aside and conversed with her privately for a long while, then brought her back to her mother and husband. Before they left, St. Seraphim bowed to Pelagia and instructed her mother to take her to Diveyevo so that she could "defend my orphans" there. He then gave her a prayer rope and bade them farewell. After they left, a young monk asked St. Seraphim who this strange woman was, and Seraphim replied, "Believe God, Father Ivan, this woman whom you see will be a great luminary for the whole world."[46]

After returning home with her husband, Pelagia's behavior remained unchanged, and she began again walking the streets nearly naked and spending all night in prayer on the church porch. Whenever Sergei would try to help her by giving her warm clothing or money for her needs, she would immediately turn around and give away these things to the poor. This eventually became more than Sergei could bear, and so he turned her out. Pelagia then returned to her mother's house, but there she continued suffering beatings and mistreatment from her stepfather and half-siblings.

In desperation, Pelagia's mother went again to visit St. Seraphim to see what might be done, and he instructed her to allow Pelagia to continue acting in whatever way she chose, as it was pleasing to God. After that, Pelagia was allowed to live as she desired without being chastised or punished.

---

46   Anonymous, *Seraphim's Seraphim*, 7.

After St. Seraphim reposed in 1837, a nun from Diveyevo went to Pelagia's home and asked her mother for permission to bring her to the monastery. This was granted, and Pelagia was received in Diveyevo as a "mad fool." There she continued her bizarre behaviors, living on the streets in a pit filled with filth and sometimes banging her head intentionally on the monastery walls. She even drove nails into her bare feet and lived on nothing but bread and water. It wasn't unusual for some of the nuns to abuse her with taunts and blows, since they did not comprehend her calling. But other sisters did understand and venerated her, so that her reputation for "holy madness" spread abroad.

Pelagia was blessed with the gift of healing and would have compassion on those who came to her. Among those she healed was the artist Michael Petrovich Petrov who suffered from paralysis of the hand.[47] She also had the gift of clairvoyance (a frequent gift granted to many fools for Christ), and she sometimes would appear to people in their dreams. Petrov, who once had visited Pelagia in the monastery when she was ill, related that when he himself became gravely ill from diphtheria he longed for Pelagia to come visit him in his misery, but she did not. After bemoaning his lonely estate one night he fell asleep, and in a dream Pelagia stood near him and said, "There, now I have come to visit you; don't be afraid, you won't die."[48] And soon thereafter he did indeed recover from his illness.

Petrov also related the following story about the saint: The two once were drinking tea together, and just as tea was being poured into Pelagia's cup she suddenly jumped up from the floor and hastily ran out with the cup. Once outside, she poured the contents of the cup in the direction of a nearby village. The next day a woman from that village came to see Pelagia and prostrated herself at the saint's feet,

---

47   The full account of Michael Petrov can be found in *Seraphim's Seraphim,*
      105–113.
48   *Seraphim's Seraphim,* 109.

thanking her for saving her house. It seems that a fire had started in her barn the night before, and the wheat stored inside was beginning to burn. She related that she cried out in desperation, "Matushka Pelagia Ivanovna, save us!"[49] and immediately the wind changed direction and blew the fire away from the grain, and it quickly went out. Petrov noted that the woman said the wind changed and the fire went out at exactly the same time Pelagia had poured out her tea into the street the night before.

Because of incidents like these, Pelagia's fame became widely known, and she received visitors from all across Russia and from every walk of life.

After she had spent twenty years in asceticism, Pelagia received a vision of St. Seraphim in a dream. Exactly what he counseled her is not known, but following that, Pelagia shut herself in a cell and avoided seeing people. She practiced silence and would sit and sleep on the bare floor of her cell next to the door, spending all night in prayer. She would eat only black bread, which she rolled into little balls and used as a prayer rope to count her prayers. Thus she lived until her death on January 30, 1884.

Shortly before she reposed, a nun witnessed angels surrounding Pelagia and communing her with the Holy Mysteries. Pelagia became known as the "Second Seraphim" or "Seraphim's Seraphim."

---

49   *Seraphim's Seraphim*, 109.

St. Prokopiy of Ustyug
(ca. 1243-1303)

T HE EXACT DATE AND PLACE of Prokopiy's birth are not known, but he was a foreigner (most likely a German) of the Roman Catholic confession. As a merchant, he traded often in Novgorod, where he was exposed to the beauty of Holy Orthodoxy. After observing the depth of Orthodox worship, he renounced papism and converted to the Orthodox faith.

Though he had acquired substantial wealth as a merchant, once his heart was converted he chose to give away all his possessions to the poor and became a monk at the St. Varlaam of Khutyn Monastery near Novgorod. Word spread throughout the city of this rich foreigner who divested himself of all his great wealth, converted to Orthodoxy, and became a humble monk. His name grew to be highly praised among the people, but such acclaim displeased Prokopiy, as he knew this would tempt him to pride and vainglory. He believed that the people should direct their praise only to God. So, after a time he left the monastery and relocated to Ustyug, where no one knew him, and took up the difficult podvig of being a fool for Christ. (Some postulate that Prokopiy may have been the first fool for Christ in Russia, patterning his struggles after those of St. Andrew of Constantinople—see pages 9–13).

There in Ustyug, Prokopiy endeavored to conquer pride and adopt true humility. Possessing nothing but three wooden staffs, he wandered barefoot and poorly clad through the city streets in both summer and winter. When he was tired, he often would rest on a pile of manure, and at night he typically slept on a church porch or even out in the open. He would accept alms from those with meager possessions, but he would refuse any offered to him by the wealthy, believing that the rich likely obtained their wealth through immoral means. The local citizens misunderstood him, and they would daily mock, insult, spit upon, and sometimes even beat him as he walked about. At night he would spend much time in prayer, supplicating especially for those who had abused him during the day, echoing the words of the Savior, "Father, forgive them, for they do not know what they do" (Luke 23:34).

One day when the winter weather was even more bitterly cold than usual—so cold that it was said birds would freeze in flight—Prokopiy sought shelter but could find none. Every place where he asked for haven turned him away. Finally he decided to warm himself by lying down amongst a pack of dogs that roamed the streets, but even the dogs fled away from him. Accepting that this must be the hour of his death, he, like Job, blessed the Lord and lay down to wait for God to take his soul. But suddenly he saw an angel beside him holding a branch from Paradise in his hand. The angel touched Prokopiy's brow with it, and he felt a wave of warmth embrace his entire body. Thus he was saved from a death by freezing, and he related this incident to his priest with the admonition that the priest never tell anyone about it until after his repose.

For his great struggles, the Lord blessed Prokopiy with the gifts of wonderworking and clairvoyance. He often would see people's future life and encourage them on a righteous path. Once he bowed down before a three-year-old girl and said, "Here is the mother of a great saint."[50] Of course, this was perceived at the time as foolishness, for certainly no child so young could be a mother. But in time the girl grew up to marry and give birth to the future notable hierarch Stephen of Perm.

In the year 1290, Prokopiy's behavior grew even more shocking to the people of Ustyug. During Liturgy one Sunday he shouted out, "Repent of your sins, brethren! Hurry to please God by fasting and prayers, or else the city will be ruined by a fiery hail!"[51] After the people derided him for interrupting the Liturgy and ignored his message, he went out onto the church porch and wept bitterly throughout the rest of the day and into the night. For the next few days, he went about the streets of the city weeping and crying out, "Keep vigil and pray that you do not fall into disaster! Weep friends! Weep about your prayers; pray that the Lord might deliver you from the anger of the truth, that it might not destroy you like Sodom and Gomorrah because of your transgressions!"[52]

Even so, most of the people merely thought the beggar mad and paid little attention to him. But a few days later a black cloud appeared in the sky at a distance and began making its way toward the city. Lightning flashed from the cloud, and there was boisterous thunder

---

50   "St. Procopius, Fool-for-Christ, Wonderworker of Ustiug."
51   Novakshonoff, *God's Fools*, 56.
52   Novakshonoff, 57.

beyond what anyone had ever heard before. Suddenly the people remembered Prokopiy's pleas and ran en masse to the Cathedral of the Theotokos. Here they found Prokopiy already there, weeping and praying for the people in front of the icon of the Annunciation. The people began following suit, weeping for their sins and begging God for forgiveness and deliverance.

Abruptly, myrrh began to flow from the icon, and the atmosphere both within and without the cathedral changed. Instead of a heavy, stifling presence, the air in the cathedral became filled with a glorious fragrance. The cloud approaching the city moved away in the opposite direction, and the city was rescued from almost certain destruction. Later it was discovered that in addition to the tremendously destructive storm that produced deadly hail, lightning, and tornadoes, a meteorite also had struck the forest just outside of Ustyug, doing considerable damage and, along with the copious lightning, started a large forest fire. The calamity destroyed many of the ancient trees in the forest, but miraculously no harm came to either humans or beasts anywhere in the region.

The people, having repented of their wicked behaviors, turned back to serving God with their whole hearts. The myrrh that streamed from the icon of the Annunciation was so profuse it filled all the vessels in the church. Those who were anointed with the myrrh found healing from various ailments.

It is said that every word that proceeded from the mouth of Prokopiy was full of exhortation and admonition about leading a virtuous life. Having fulfilled his struggles in a manner well-pleasing to the Lord, Prokopiy fell asleep in Christ on July 8, 1303, at about sixty years of age. His incorrupt relics were discovered near the Entry of the Theotokos parish in the eighteenth century. Today in Ustyug there is a cathedral dedicated to the memory of the righteous

Prokopiy, and it sits atop one of the steep hills along the Sukhona River. It is said that this site was chosen because it was on this hill that the meteorite fell during the storm of 1290. And it was from this storm that St. Prokopiy's prayers helped save the city. He continues to pray for all people, and many miracles have been recorded as having been worked through the saint since his repose.

St. Symeon of Emesa
(sixth century)

MOST OF THE LIVES OF fools for Christ appear to be extraordinary and even controversial—especially to the world—but that of Symeon of Emesa is one of the most complex and unusual of all. One of the earliest-recorded holy fools of Christendom, Symeon remains a complicated figure to this day.

Born around the year 522 in Edessa, he was reportedly of noble and certainly wealthy lineage. Little is known of his early life in Edessa, but he is known to have set out on a pilgrimage to Jerusalem around age thirty. Along the way he befriended a fellow pilgrim also from Edessa named John who would become his lifelong friend and confidant. After celebrating the Exaltation of the Cross in Jerusalem together, the two returned to their respective homes in Edessa but remained close friends, both devoted wholeheartedly to following God.

Though both Symeon and John were quite wealthy, they gave up all their earthly inheritance in exchange for an inheritance above, and they both entered the Monastery of St. Gerasimos where they were tonsured monks. After about a year there, the two left the monastery for the desert near the Dead Sea. There they spent the better part of the next thirty years in solitude and prayer, struggling to overcome all earthly passions.

When Symeon was about sixty years of age, he received inspiration from God to return to the world and go to Emesa in order to provide aid and guidance to the people there. Symeon asked the Lord if he might be allowed to serve the people in a way that would bring no glory or praise to himself, so that all might know whatever good he may perform would be done only by the hand of God who alone should receive praise. Thus, when he arrived in Emesa, Symeon took on the difficult role of playing a fool for Christ's sake, in order that all might think him mad and attribute all good things to God alone.

He began his role when he first reached the city gates of Emesa. Just outside the gates he found a dead dog lying on a heap of refuse. Taking the rope from around his pallium, he tied one end to the dog's leg and the other around his waist so that he entered the city dragging the carcass of the dog behind him. He achieved the goal of simulating madness right from his first moments in Emesa, as when he entered dragging the dead dog a group of boys taunted him by calling out, "Hey! A dumb monk!"[53] and cuffing him on the head.

The next day was Sunday, and Symeon entered the church for the Liturgy and behaved like a madman there as well, extinguishing lampadas, and cracking walnuts with his hands and throwing the shells at women in the church. When he was chased out of the sanctuary

---

53   Leontius, *St. Symeon*, 84.

for such behavior, he overturned the tables of the pastry bakers who had set up shop next to the church doors—similar to what Jesus had done to the money changers in the Temple. For doing this the bakers attacked and beat Symeon severely.

Once when Symeon wished to offer incense at his evening prayers, he looked about but could find no lamp or even a piece of pottery to use. Instead he simply reached his hand into the burning coals and offered the incense in his hand without harm. When someone observed this, he quickly pretended to have burned his hand, and he put the coals and incense in the folds of his pallium . . . but like the bush before Moses or the holy youths in the fiery furnace, the fire did not harm the fabric at all.

So ardent was he that no glory or praise should be given to himself that anytime he performed unusual acts like this he would immediately leave the neighborhood where they had occurred and not return until the events were forgotten. He even would cease from doing anything that might draw attention to himself and bring him praise, lest he be led to any degree of pride. Hence, his acts of madness and even seeming effrontery were designed to draw praise away from himself, and he would intentionally act so as to be thought insane rather than have people think of him as being holy. He purposely chose to be thought a fool in order to conceal his own identity as a saint.

Symeon would cast off his mask of foolishness for only one person, his dear friend Deacon John, and he would converse with him in a totally rational fashion, clearly revealing that playing the fool was a deliberate act. Even while playing the fool, Symeon healed many people by his prayers, fed the hungry, and preached the gospel of Christ. And while his biographer, St. Leontius of Cyprus, recorded many of his deeds, no doubt exponentially more were done in secret and are known only to God.

During his days in Emesa, Symeon engaged in a number of different "odd jobs." Once he worked as a hot-water boy in a tavern,

performing his task well despite the harsh treatment he received from
the tavern owner who often would not even give him food. One day
a serpent got into one of the wine vessels unnoticed and poisoned
the wine. When Symeon entered the tavern, he saw with his spiritual
sight the word "death" inscribed on the vessel. He therefore smashed
the flagon to bits, preventing any of the patrons from drinking the
poisonous wine. The tavern owner was unaware of why Symeon had
done this and, taking the stick with which Symeon had broken the
flagon, began beating him with it until Symeon fled. It wasn't until
the tavern owner saw the serpent return the next day that he understood what had happened and that Symeon had been gifted with spiritual insight in order to save the patrons.

In addition to saving the lives of people about him, Symeon also
led many to repentance, thereby saving their eternal lives from
destruction. He would cry out against thieves and fornicators and
others who fell from righteous living.

On one occasion a troupe of mimes came to town. (During this
time period, mimes were traveling performers who often depicted
obscene acts on stage and were noted for their sinful and loose life-
styles.) When one of the mimes, a juggler, was about to perform
a lewd act, Symeon picked up a small pebble, made the sign of the
cross over it, and threw it at the juggler, hitting him on the hand. No
one saw him do this, but suddenly the juggler's right hand withered
and was paralyzed. He did not know what had happened to him until
one night Symeon appeared to him in a dream and told him that it
was he who had hit him with the pebble. Symeon then said to him,
"[A]nd unless you swear that you will never try such a thing again,
you will not get well."[54] The mime swore to Symeon by the Theotokos
that he would never do such a trick again, and when he awoke from
the dream he found his hand fully restored. When he later described

_____
54   Leontius, 95.

all that had happened to him, he himself did not know it had been Symeon in the dream but said it was "Some monk or other wearing a wreath made out of palm-leaves."[55]

He also once chastised the son of Deacon John for secretly committing adultery with a married woman and thereby entertaining the demon of lust. Symeon found him and, wishing to make him chaste and lead him to repentance, gave him a blow to the jaw shouting, "Never commit adultery again, you miserable wretch; then the demon won't come near you."[56] At this, the demon cast Deacon John's son to the ground, and as he lay foaming at the mouth, he saw Symeon chase a black dog out of him, beating it with a wooden cross.

Many other wonders (and eccentricities) Symeon performed are recorded. Blessed with the gift of clairvoyance, as many fools for Christ seem to have been, he foretold the great earthquake of 588 that flattened Antioch and did much damage throughout the region. Prior to the quake, Symeon took a whip about town, striking various pillars and saying to some, "Thy Lord hath said: 'Stand!'" and to others, "Thou, neither fall nor stand."[57] The people once more thought all this was just the action of a madman, but after the earthquake they observed that all the pillars he had told to stand remained upright, and those to which he had said "neither stand nor fall" had been split from top to bottom or were leaning at an angle.

At one point Symeon was accused of having impregnated a local housemaid, though he was completely innocent. Rather than denying the charge, he pretended to be the father and cared lovingly for the pregnant maid, even calling her "my wife." When the time came for her to deliver the baby, she was in heavy labor for three days and nearing the point of death. The mistress of the house bade Symeon to pray for the young woman, and so, behaving foolishly, he clapped

---

55   Leontius, 95.
56   Leontius, 93.
57   Leontius, 96.

his hands and danced around her crying, "[T]he child won't come out from there until she tells who the father is!"[58] Hearing that, the girl confessed that she had falsely accused Symeon and then named the actual father. After that she immediately gave birth. Some present then thought Symeon was a saint while others insisted that because he was a fool he divined truth by sorcery and witchcraft.

On another occasion a Jewish journeyman of the city wished to reveal Symeon's saintliness publicly because he had witnessed two angels conversing with Symeon as he was bathing one day. Before he could fulfill his mission, Symeon appeared to him in a dream at night and commanded him not to tell anyone what he had seen. Determined the next morning to expose Symeon regardless, as the journeyman was on his way to make the proclamation he saw Symeon suddenly standing next to him. Symeon touched his lips, and the journeyman was immediately rendered mute and could not speak at all. The Jew then made signs to Symeon that he wished to be healed. True to fashion, Symeon played the fool with him and made silly signs back to him, but eventually convinced him that he would not be healed until he was baptized a Christian. The Jew did not concede until after Symeon had died, but when he was baptized he was able to speak again immediately as he came up from the font (more about this on the next page).

Symeon was able to keep inordinately strict fasts, but at times he would allow himself to be seen publicly eating freely on certain fast days. For instance, he would eat nothing at all during the forty days of Great Lent, but then on Holy Thursday he would sit and eat openly at the pastry cook's café. At other times he would eat huge quantities of beans on a strict fast day, producing the foreseeable results to others' disgust.

Throughout his days as a fool for Christ, most who knew Symeon saw him as a madman—Deacon John alone knew the full breadth of his holiness. As one author put it, he was "a secret saint," his story "a holy farce,"[59] his life showing that God indeed chooses "the foolish things of the world to put to shame the wise; and God has chosen the weak things of the world to put to shame the things which are mighty" (1 Cor. 1:27).

For three days before his death, Symeon did not appear on the streets but remained in his hut—a humble habitation that held nothing but a cot made of twigs and branches and a pile of firewood. It was where Symeon would pass each night in prayer, and for those three days before his repose he spent day and night so engaged. After three days some of the locals thought to check in on him, and when they entered his hut they found him lying peacefully asleep in the Lord, not on his cot but underneath it, as though playing the fool even in death.

The men who found him picked up his body and carried it to the local potter's field where the poor and homeless were buried. As they carried the body through the streets, people heard choirs of angels pass by in heavenly chorus while a wondrous fragrance filled the air. Among those who heard this heavenly choir was the Jewish journeyman who had been struck dumb by Symeon, and as he observed the holy procession he decided to accept Christian baptism as did his entire house later.

Saint Symeon's friend Deacon John preserved his life and deeds and passed them on to his biographer. Symeon passed from this life on July 21, probably in the year 590. Deacon John sought to retrieve his relics from the potter's field for a more proper burial, but when his coffin was located and opened they found no body inside—God had already translated his holy body to the heavenly Kingdom. It was only after his death that Symeon's secret life came to light and he was revealed as a great saint of God.

---

59   "St Simeon the Holy Fool."

St. Xenia of St. Petersburg (eighteenth century)

M UCH OF ST. XENIA'S LIFE remains a mystery as we know neither the dates of her birth nor of her death, but only that she lived in eighteenth-century Russia. (Some speculate that her birth year was 1731, but nothing is known for certain about her origins.) It would seem that she led a rather comfortable life, and it is known that she was happily married and devoted to her husband, Col. Andrei Feodorovich Petrov, a chanter in the imperial court.

When she was twenty-six years of age, her husband died suddenly, by some accounts as a result of over-imbibing at a drinking party. Inconsolable in her grief at her husband's death, she turned her heart entirely to contemplating the Kingdom of heaven and disdained anything of the world. Giving away all her personal possessions to the poor, she threw off all ties to worldly things. She even gave away her own house to a friend, Paraskeva Antonova, with the provision that she use the house to offer shelter for the poor.

When relatives saw her homeless, they offered to assist her by providing refuge and other amenities, but she always refused, insisting that she needed nothing of this world. Some of her relatives assumed she had gone mad from grief, and they even sought help from the trustees of her husband's estate to have her pronounced mentally incompetent. But after examining her, the trustees ruled that she was entirely in possession of all her faculties and had the right to determine the disposition of her property on her own.

Once she had divested herself of all her belongings, Xenia disappeared from St. Petersburg for a time. It is not known where she was during this time, but it is believed that she may have spent those eight years in a convent of ascetics where she learned about spiritual life and the prayer of the heart and where she further advanced her desire to be a fool for Christ.

When she returned to St. Petersburg, she dressed herself in her husband's military uniform and insisted that others address her by the name Andrei Feodorovich rather than Xenia. Taking upon herself the ascesis of foolishness for Christ, she commenced wandering the streets and fields in and around St. Petersburg, focusing all her life on God and often praying throughout the night. It is thought that she saw wearing her late husband's attire as an attempt to help take upon herself any of his unforgiven sins, considering the manner he had passed from this life. It was as though whatever good deeds she did were done, as it were, by Andrei Feodorovich rather than by the fool Xenia.

The people of St. Petersburg initially looked askance at this oddly dressed woman and considered her a simpleminded beggar who associated with riffraff and paupers. Some cruel citizens and unruly street urchins persecuted her and laughed at her foolish ways. In response

to these taunts, the blessed one exhibited only meekness and forgiveness, showing herself to be an icon of the Lord Himself who suffered
at the hands of evil men.

In all her life, there is only one instance recorded of Xenia ever
becoming angry. Apparently, one day in the Petrogradskaya Storona
district some young hoodlums berated her and mocked her inces-
santly. In response St. Xenia maintained her patient meekness and
ignored them. But finding their taunts ineffective, the lads resorted to
throwing mud and rocks at her instead. At this Xenia finally stormed
at the young ruffians, waving her cane in the air. So unusual was
this occurrence that the boys fled, and those who witnessed it were
so taken aback that they made certain no one would bother the holy
woman again.

In time the people of St. Petersburg grew to see Xenia not as a
beggar but as someone quite special. Many people, even among the
higher classes, often would invite her into their homes for tea and to
offer her warm clothing and alms. Xenia would never accept the offer
of clothing or any money of substance but would allow them to give
her only small copper pennies that were called "the tsar on horseback." It is thought that she would accept these because they depicted
a horseman, which reminded her of her late husband.

But even these pennies she did not keep for herself but would distribute them to the poor. Having been blessed with the gift of clairvoyance, she sometimes would give away these coins along with some
prophetic advice. Once, for instance, she met a devout woman on
the street and pressed a coin into her hand saying, "Take this [coin].
Here is the king on horseback; it will be extinguished."[60] The woman
accepted the coin and went on her way, puzzled by the holy woman's words. As she came to the street on which she lived, she saw that
there was a fire in one of the houses. Rushing toward it, she saw that it

---

60 Anonymous, *Life and Miracles*, 10.

was her own house that was ablaze, but she arrived just in time to see the flames being fully extinguished.

Exactly when in her ascesis Blessed Xenia received the gift of clairvoyance is not known, just as so many other events in her life are not recorded. But it became well known throughout St. Petersburg that she possessed this special gift that allowed her to witness for Christ.

On one occasion Xenia went to visit her friend Paraskeva Antonova in the house she had given to her. She found Paraskeva sewing. Xenia looked at her irritably and said, "Here you are sitting and sewing on buttons and you don't know that God has given you a son! Go at once to the Smolensk Cemetery!"[61]

Though Paraskeva had not a clue what Xenia meant by these words, she knew her friend well enough to know that she did not speak idle words. And so, without questioning Xenia, she hastened to the Smolensk cemetery, not knowing what she would find there. When she arrived she noticed a crowd of people assembled on a nearby street. Curious as to what was happening, she approached them to learn that a coachman had run over a pregnant woman who immediately gave birth right in the street and then died. Filled with compassion for the newborn child, Paraskeva took the infant to her own home to care for him until his father or other relative could be found. But all attempts to locate a family member of the child were unsuccessful, and so she brought the lad up as her son, and he was a great blessing to her.

On another occasion Xenia was visiting with a Mrs. Golubev, who had a seventeen-year-old daughter whom Xenia favored because of her meekness and kind nature. As this daughter was making coffee for their guest, Xenia said to her, "My beauty, here you are making coffee and your husband is burying his wife in Okhta. Run there quickly!"[62] At Xenia's insistence the young girl finally was convinced

---

61   Novakshonoff, *God's Fools*, 175.
62   Anonymous, *Life and Miracles*, 11.

to go to Okhta with her mother, even though she protested that she had no husband. When they arrived they found a funeral procession passing by and joined in with the other mourners. As it turned out, the young wife of a medical doctor had died in childbirth and was being buried. After the grave had been covered, the widowed husband was so grief-stricken that he collapsed beside the grave. Mrs. Golubev and her daughter sought to assist him, and in the course of time they became friends and later, the daughter became the doctor's wife.

The saint also revealed how she understood and felt compassion for those in difficult marital situations. Once when Xenia visited Evdokiya Denisievna Gaidukova, Evdokiya set out various leftovers for her to eat, apologizing for having nothing else in the house since she had not prepared anything that day. Xenia was humbly grateful for the food and thanked Evdokiya profusely, but then she said, "only why not tell the truth? You were afraid to give me some duck!"[63]

Evdokiya was surprised by Xenia's foresight, because in fact she had a roast duck in her oven that she was preparing for her husband who was expected home from a trip. Embarrassed, she started immediately for the kitchen, but Xenia stopped her, saying, "I don't want any duck. I know very well that you are happy to offer me whatever you have, but you are afraid of your mare's head. Why anger him?"[64] ("Mare's head" is what Xenia called Evdokiya's husband because she did not like his drunken and abusive character. She refused the duck in order not to agitate the husband further.)

Because of these events in the saint's life, young people often appeal to St. Xenia in prayer to help them find a mate and also for aid in restoring a broken or damaged marital relationship.

---

63   Novakshonoff, 183.
64   Novakshonoff, 183ff.

Because over time the blessed Xenia was discovered to be a holy soul, the people of St. Petersburg looked forward to giving her whatever aid they could—this despite the fact that they sometimes still could not fathom some of her "foolish" antics. In 1761, two days before the Nativity feast, Xenia was seen running through the streets shouting, "Bake bliny! Bake bliny! Soon all of Russia will be baking bliny!"[65] (Bliny is a Russian pancake that at the time was traditionally served at wakes for the recently deceased.)

Of course, no one could understand the meaning behind this odd behavior, but then on the first day of the feast, the Empress Elisabeth Petrovna died suddenly and unexpectedly. As the news spread throughout the country, the meaning of Xenia's prophetic utterance became clear.

For a long time, no one knew where Xenia spent her nights. She could be seen wandering the streets and fields during daylight, but she seemed just to disappear after sunset. The police investigated the situation and found that she would spend her nights in an open field, praying and making prostrations all through the night. Despite being exposed to the elements and wearing nothing but worn-out clothing, she nevertheless survived even the bitter winter St. Petersburg nights in this fashion, seemingly no worse for it.

Near the end of the saint's earthly life, a church was being built in the Smolensk cemetery. The construction workers noticed that during the night, while they were all home asleep, someone would move large bundles of bricks to the top of the building where they were needed the next day. Curious to know what charitable crew was moving such heavy material for them, the workers posted a watchman one night to discover whom to thank. They were amazed to learn that it was the aged Xenia who would move the bricks for them, granted the strength to do so by an unseen Hand.

---

65   Pehanich, "St. Xenia of St. Petersburg, Russia."

Sometime around the end of the eighteenth century or the beginning of the nineteenth, the citizens of St. Petersburg noticed that Xenia was no longer wandering the streets of their city, nor could they find her in the field she frequented at night. God had called the holy laborer to Himself, granting her rest from her many labors. As a fool for Christ, she had given up living for herself and had lived for others. She was buried in the Smolensk cemetery where many wondrous acts are recorded at her grave even to this very day.

OTHER FOOLS FOR CHRIST AND THEIR FEAST DAYS

Alexander of Cosmas	August 12
Anastasia Andreyevna	March 1
Andrew of Simbirsk	November 27
Anthony of Valaam	June 7
Anthony of Zadonsk	September 29
Arsenius of Novgorod	July 12
Asenatha of Goritsky	April 19
Athanasius of Orel	April 12
Cosmas of Verkhoturye	November 1
Cyprian of Suzdal	October 2
George of Shenkursk	April 23
John of Moscow	July 3
John of Tula	January 12
John of Verkhoturye	April 16
John the Barefooted of Kiev	December 16
John the Hairy of Rostov	September 3
Jonah of Peshnosha Monastery	June 15
Lawrence of Kaluga	August 10
Matrona of Anemnyasevo	July 29
Maximus of Moscow	November 11
Maximus of Mt. Athos	January 13

Maximus of Totma	January 16
Paisius of the Kiev Caves	April 17
Parasceva of Starobelsk	October 17
Paraskeva of the Balkans	October 14
Pimen & Anthony of Meskhi	March 16
Prokopiy of Vyatka	December 21
Simon of Yurievetz & Zharki	November 4
Theodore of Novgorod	January 19
Theoktista of Voronezh	February 22
Theophil of Sviatogorsk	January 30
Thomas of Syria	April 24
Timothy of Svyatogorsk	July 17

RECOMMENDED READING

Anonymous. *The Life and Miracles of Blessed Xenia of St. Petersburg.* Jordanville, NY: Holy Trinity Monastery Printshop of St. Job of Pochaev, 1997.

Anonymous. *Seraphim's Seraphim: The Life of Pelagia Ivanovna Serebrenikova, Fool for Christ's Sake of the Seraphim-Diveyevo Convent.* Boston: Holy Transfiguration Monastery, 1978.

Leontius. *Saint Symeon of Emesa.* Boston: Holy Transfiguration Monastery, 2014.

Novakshonoff, Varlaam. *God's Fools: The Lives of the Holy "Fools for Christ."* Dewdney, BC, Canada: Synaxis Press, 2017.

Velimirovic, Nikolai. *The Prologue of Ohrid.* 3rd ed. Alhambra, CA: Sebastian Press, 2017.

Znosko, Vladimir. *Hieroschemamonk Feofil: Fool-for-Christ's-Sake.* Jordanville, NY: Holy Trinity Monastery Printshop of St. Job of Pochaev, 1998.

BIBLIOGRAPHY

Introduction

Doherty, Catherine. *Uródivoi*. Combermere, Ontario, Canada: Madonna House, 2021.

Bajis, Jordan. *Common Ground*. Minneapolis: Light and Life Publishing, 1989.

St. Andrew of Constantinople

Ancient Faith Ministries. "St Andrew the Fool for Christ." *Saint of the Day.* October 2, 2019. Podcast. https://www.ancientfaith.com/podcasts/saintof theday/st_andrew_the_fool_for_christ_911.

Novakshonoff, Varlaam. *God's Fools: The Lives of the Holy "Fools for Christ."* Dewdney, BC, Canada: Synaxis Press, 2017.

Orthodox Church in America. "Blessed Andrew the Fool-For-Christ at Constantinople." https://www.oca.org/saints/lives/2025/10/02/102838 -blessed-andrew-the-fool-for-christ-at-constantinople.

Orthodox Wiki. "Andrew the Fool-for-Christ." Last modified November 28, 2018. https://orthodoxwiki.org/Andrew_the_Fool-for-Christ.

St. Andrew of Totma

Ancient Faith Ministries. "Blessed Fool for Christ Andrew of Totma." *Saint of the Day.* October 10, 2017. Podcast. https://www.ancientfaith.com/podcasts /saintoftheday/blessed_fool_for_christ_andrew_of_totma4.

Novakshonoff, Varlaam. *God's Fools: The Lives of the Holy "Fools for Christ."* Dewdney, BC, Canada: Synaxis Press, 2017.

Sanidopoulos, John. "Saint Andrew of Totma the Fool for Christ." *Orthodox Christianity Then and Now* (blog), October 10, 2018. https://www .johnsanidopoulos.com/2018/10/saint-andrew-of-totma-fool-for-christ .html.

St. Basil of Moscow

Manaev, Georgy. "Blessed Basil, the Man Who Got Away with Scolding Ivan the Terrible." *Russia Beyond*. December 12, 2017. https://www.rbth.com /history/327004-blessed-basil.

———. "Why Did Russian Tsars Love 'Holy Fools?'" *Russia Beyond*. January 21, 2020. https://www.rbth.com/history/331573-why-did-russian-tsars-love.

Novakshonoff, Varlaam. *God's Fools: The Lives of the Holy "Fools for Christ."* Dewdney, BC, Canada: Synaxis Press, 2017.

Orthodox Church in America. "Blessed Basil of Moscow the Fool-For-Christ." www.oca.org/saints/lives/1999/08/02/102185-blessed-basil-of-moscow -the-fool-for-christ.

St. Domna of Tomsk

Orthodox Church in America. "Saint Domna of Tomsk." https://www.oca.org /saints/lives/2022/10/16/105703-saint-domna-of-tomsk.

Sanidopoulos, John. "Saint Domna of Tomsk, the Fool for Christ." *Orthodox Christianity Then and Now* (blog), October 16, 2017. https://www .johnsanidopoulos.com/2017/10/saint-domna-of-tomsk-fool-for-christ .html.

St. Feofil of the Kiev Caves

Orthodox Christianity. "The Life of St. Feofil, Fool-for-Christ of Kiev." November 10, 2021. https://orthochristian.com/142818.html.

Sanidopoulos, John. "Saint Feofil of the Kiev Caves, the Fool for Christ." *Orthodox Christianity Then and Now* (blog), October 28, 2017. https://www.john sanidopoulos.com/2017/10/saint-feofil-of-kiev-caves-fool-for.html.

Znosko, Vladimir. *Hieroschemamonk Feofil: Fool-for-Christ's-Sake*. Jordanville, NY: Holy Trinity Monastery Printshop of St. Job of Pochaev, 1998.

Bibliography

St. Gabriel of Mtskheta

Khrustalyeva, Larisa. "Elder Gabriel (Urgebadze): His Life, Miracles, and Service After His Death." *Orthodox Christianity*. November 19, 2013. https://orthochristian.com/65883.html.

Obitel-Minsk Team. "Saint Gabriel of Samtavro, Georgia's Beloved Modern Saint." St. Elisabeth Convent. August 24, 2023. https://obitel-minsk.org/en/saint-gabriel-of-samtavro-georgias-beloved-modern-saint.

Pehanich, Edward. "St. Gabriel Urgebadze." American Carpatho-Russian Orthodox Diocese of North America. https://www.acrod.org/orthodox-christianity/articles/saints/st-gregory-urgebadze.

Sanidopoulos, John. "Saint Gabriel the Confessor and Fool for Christ." *Orthodox Christianity Then and Now* (blog), November 2, 2017. https://www.johnsanidopoulos.com/2017/11/saint-gabriel-confessor-and-fool-for.html.

Transfiguration Orthodox Church of Samtavro and Convent of St. Nino. "Archimandrite Gabriel Urgebadze, 1929–1995: Life and Works." https://monkgabriel.ge/eng/life.htm.

St. Isidora of Tabenna

Ancient Faith Ministries. "Apostle Simon Zelotes and St Isidora the Fool of Tabenna." *Saint of the Day.* May 9, 2010. Podcast. https://www.ancientfaith.com/podcasts/saintoftheday/may_10_-_apostle_simon_zelotes_and_st_isidora_the_fool_of_tabenna.

Novakshonoff, Varlaam. *God's Fools: The Lives of the Holy "Fools for Christ."* Dewdney, BC, Canada: Synaxis Press, 2017.

Puhalo, Lazar. *Lives of Saints for Young People,* vol. 12. CreateSpace Independent Publishing, 2018.

Sanidopoulos, John. "Venerable Isidora the Fool for Christ of Tabennisi." *Orthodox Christianity Then and Now* (blog), May 1, 2018. https://www.johnsanidopoulos.com/2018/05/venerable-isidora-fool-for-christ-of.html.

St. Isidore of Rostov

Ancient Faith Ministries. "Blessed Isidore the Fool for Christ." *Saint of the Day.* May 14, 2023. Podcast. https://www.ancientfaith.com/podcasts/saintoftheday/blessed_isidore_the_fool_for_christ_14841.

Novakshonoff, Varlaam. *God's Fools: The Lives of the Holy "Fools for Christ."* Dewdney, BC, Canada: Synaxis Press, 2017.

Orthodox Church in America. "Venerable Isidore the Fool-For-Christ and Wonderworker of Rostov." https://www.oca.org/saints/lives/2023/05/14/101376-venerable-isidore-the-fool-for-christ-and-wonderworker-of-rostov.

Sanidopoulos, John. "Saint Isidore of Rostov the Fool for Christ." *Orthodox Christianity Then and Now* (blog), May 13, 2011. https://www.johnsanidopoulos.com/2011/05/saint-isidore-of-rostov-fool-for-christ.html.

St. John of Ustyug

Novakshonoff, Varlaam. *God's Fools: The Lives of the Holy "Fools for Christ."* Dewdney, BC, Canada: Synaxis Press, 2017.

Sanidopoulos, John. "Saint John of Ustiug the Fool for Christ." *Orthodox Christianity Then and Now* (blog), May 29, 2020. https://www.johnsanidopoulos.com/2020/05/saint-john-of-ustiug-fool-for-christ.html.

St. Lyubov of Ryazan

Orthodox Church in America. "Blessed Liubov (Sukhanovskaya) of Ryazan, Fool for Christ." https://www.oca.org/saints/lives/2022/02/08/100321-blessed-liubov-sukhanovskaya-of-ryazan-fool-for-christ.

Sanidopoulos, John. "Saint Lyubov of Ryazan, the Fool for Christ." *Orthodox Christianity Then and Now* (blog), February 8, 2020. https://www.johnsanidopoulos.com/2020/02/saint-lyubov-of-ryazan-fool-for-christ.html.

St. Maria of Diveyevo

Orthodox Christianity. "Blessed Maria Ivanovna of Diveyevo." October 8, 2011. https://orthochristian.com/48442.html.

St. Nicholas Russian Orthodox Church, McKinney Texas. "Monastic Martyrs and Confessors of Sarov and Diveyevo." https://www.orthodox.net/russiannm/sarov-and-diveyevo-monastic-martyrs-and-confessors.html.

Sanidopoulos, John. "Saint Maria Ivanovna of Diveyevo, the Fool for Christ." *Orthodox Christianity Then and Now* (blog), August 26, 2017. https://www.johnsanidopoulos.com/2017/08/saint-maria-ivanovna-of-diveyevo-fool.html.

St. Michael of Klops Monastery

Ancient Faith Ministries. "Venerable Michael of Klops, Fool for Christ." *Saint of the Day*. January 11, 2020. Podcast. https://www.ancientfaith.com/podcasts /saintoftheday/venerable_michael_of_klops_fool_for_christ_1456.

Novakshonoff, Varlaam. *God's Fools: The Lives of the Holy "Fools for Christ."* Dewdney, BC, Canada: Synaxis Press, 2017.

Orthodox Church in America. "Venerable Michael the Fool-for-Christ of the Klops Monastery, Novgorod." https://www.oca.org/saints/lives/2022/01 /11/100150-venerable-michael-the-fool-for-christ-of-the-klops-monastery -nov.

Sanidopoulos, John. "Saint Michael of Klopsk, the Fool for Christ." *Orthodox Christianity Then and Now* (blog), January 11, 2016. https://www .johnsanidopoulos.com/2016/01/saint-michael-of-klopsk-fool-for-christ .html.

St. Nicholai of Vologda

"The Wologod Saints: Righteous Nicholai Rynin." https://vk.com/wall-155175944 _3093?lang=en.

St. Nicholas of Novgorod

Esparza, Daniel. "Two Saints, a River, and a Cabbage: A Holy Fools' Story." *Aleteia*. May 14, 2023. https://aleteia.org/2023/05/14/two-saints-a-river-and-a -cabbage-a-holy-fools-story/.

Orthodox Church in America. "Blessed Nicholas Kochanov the Fool-For-Christ at Novgorod." https://www.oca.org/saints/lives/2024/07/27/102100-blessed -nicholas-kochanov-the-fool-for-christ-at-novgorod.

Orthodox Wiki. "Nicholas Konchanov of Novgorod." Last modified October 24, 2012. https://orthodoxwiki.org/Nicholas_Konchanov_of_Novgorod.

St. Nicholas of Pskov

Ancient Faith Ministries. "Blessed Nicholas of Pskov, Fool for Christ." *Saint of the Day*. February 28, 2022. Podcast. https://www.ancientfaith.com/podcasts /saintoftheday/blessed_nicholas_of_pskov_fool_for_christ_15763.

Manaev, Georgy. "Why Did Russian Tsars Love 'Holy Fools'?" *Russia Beyond*. January 21, 2020. https://www.rbth.com/history/331573-why-did-russian -tsars-love.

Novakshonoff, Varlaam. *God's Fools: The Lives of the Holy "Fools for Christ."* Dewdney, BC, Canada: Synaxis Press, 2017.

Underwood, Mark. "The Prophetic Voice of Blessed Nicholas of Pskov." Parish of the Kazan Icon of the Mother of God. March 1, 2022. https:// russianorthodoxchurchcardiff.com/nicholas-salos.

St. Paraskeva of Diveyevo

Holy Trinity Saint Seraphim-Diveyevo Monastery. "Blessed Paraskevi Ivanovna." https://diveevo-monastyr.ru/en/saints/blazhennaja-paraskeva/.

Orlovsky, Igumen Damascene. "Blessed Prascovia (Parasceva) Ivanovna of Sarov and Diveyevo." Orthodox Christianity. October 5, 2017. https:// orthochristian.com/106863.html.

Sanidopoulos, John. "Saint Paraskeva (or Pasha) Ivanovna of Sarov-Diveyevo." *Orthodox Christianity Then and Now* (blog), September 22, 2015. https:// www.johnsanidopoulos.com/2015/09/saint-paraskeva-or-pasha-ivanovna -of_22.html.

St. Pelagia of Diveyevo

Anonymous. *Seraphim's Seraphim: The Life of Pelagia Ivanovna Serebrenikova, Fool for Christ's Sake of the Seraphim-Diveyevo Convent.* Boston: Holy Transfiguration Monastery, 1978.

Holy Trinity Saint Seraphim-Diveyevo Monastery "Blessed Pelagia Ivanovna." https://diveevo-monastyr.ru/en/saints/blazhennaja-pelagija/.

Sanidopoulos, John. "Saint Pelagia the Fool for Christ of Diveyevo." *Orthodox Christianity Then and Now* (blog), January 30, 2018. https://www .johnsanidopoulos.com/2018/01/saint-pelagia-fool-for-christ-of.html.

St. Prokopiy of Ustyug

Father Alexander. "St. Procopius, the Fool-for-Christ of Ustiug." Orthodox Christianity. July 22, 2011. https://orthochristian.com/47707.html.

Novakshonoff, Varlaam. *God's Fools: The Lives of the Holy "Fools for Christ."* Dewdney, BC, Canada: Synaxis Press, 2017.

Russian Orthodox Cathedral of St. John the Baptist. "St. Procopius, Fool-for-Christ, Wonderworker of Ustiug." https://stjohndc.org/en/orthodoxy -foundation/saints/st-procopius-fool-christ-wonderworker-ustiug.

Sobolev, Gregory. "Holy Righteous Procopius of Ustiug, Wonder-Worker and Fool-for-Christ." Orthodox Christianity. July 21, 2016. https://orthochristian .com/95534.html.

St. Symeon of Emesa

Ancient Faith Ministries. "Our Righteous Fathers John and Symeon, the Fool for Christ's Sake." *Saint of the Day.* July 21, 2022. Podcast. https://www.ancientfaith.com/podcasts/saintoftheday/our_righteous_fathers_john_and_symeon_the_fool_for_christs_sake_5703.

Leontius. *Saint Symeon of Emesa.* Boston: Holy Transfiguration Monastery, 2014.

Sanidopoulos, John. "Miracles of St. Symeon the Fool in the City of Emesa." *Orthodox Christianity Then and Now* (blog), July 21, 2010. https://www.johnsanidopoulos.com/2010/07/miracles-of-st-symeon-fool-in-city-of.html.

Ship of Fools. "St Simeon the Holy Fool." https://shipoffools.com/st-simeon-the-holy-fool/.

St. Xenia of St. Petersburg

Ancient Faith Ministries. "Our Holy Mother Xenia of Petersburg, Fool for Christ." *Saint of the Day.* January 24, 2021. Podcast. https://www.ancientfaith.com/podcasts/saintoftheday/our_holy_mother_xenia_of_petersburg_fool_for_christ_18003.

Anonymous. *The Life and Miracles of Blessed Xenia of St. Petersburg.* Jordanville, NY: Holy Trinity Monastery Printshop of St. Job of Pochaev, 1997.

Khakimova, Yulia. "Blessed Xenia: How a 'Holy Fool' from St. Petersburg Became a Beloved Saint." *Russia Beyond.* February 7, 2023. https://www.rbth.com/history/335862-blessed-xenia-petersburg.

Novakshonoff, Varlaam. *God's Fools: The Lives of the Holy "Fools for Christ."* Dewdney, BC, Canada: Synaxis Press, 2017.

Pehanich, Edward. "St. Xenia of St. Petersburg, Russia." American Carpatho-Russian Orthodox Diocese of North America. https://www.acrod.org/orthodox-christianity/articles/saints/st-xenia-petersburg.

ABOUT THE AUTHOR

Oswin Craton was born and grew up in Alabama but currently lives in Indiana. He is the author of *A Journey of Fear and Joy*, which is the story of his journey to Orthodoxy from a fundamentalist Protestant background. He is known in the music world under his birth name John, and as a composer of classical music has written a number of ballets, operas, concertos, and other orchestral and chamber works that have been performed internationally. He is a member of All Saints Orthodox Church in Bloomington, Indiana. His patron saint is St. Oswin of Deira.

We hope you have enjoyed and benefited from this book. Your financial support makes it possible to continue our nonprofit ministry both in print and online. Because the proceeds from our book sales only partially cover the costs of operating **Ancient Faith Publishing** and **Ancient Faith Radio**, we greatly appreciate the generosity of our readers and listeners. Donations are tax deductible and can be made at **www.ancientfaith.com.**

To view our other publications,
please visit our website:
store.ancientfaith.com

 **ANCIENT FAITH RADIO**

Bringing you Orthodox Christian music, readings, prayers, teaching, and podcasts 24 hours a day since 2004 at
www.ancientfaith.com